© Copyright Laurie Grist 2024 - All rights reserved.

The content within this book may not be reproduced, duplicated, or transmitted without direct written permission from the author or the publisher.

Under no circumstances will any blame or legal responsibility be held against the publisher or author for any damages, reparation, or monetary loss due to the information contained within this book. Either directly or indirectly. You are responsible for your own choices, actions, and results.

<u>Legal Notice:</u>

This book is copyright-protected. This book is only for personal use. You cannot amend, distribute, sell, use, quote, or paraphrase any part of this book's content without the author's or publisher's consent.

<u>Disclaimer Notice:</u>

Please note the information contained within this document is for educational and entertainment purposes only. All effort has been expended to present accurate, up-to-date, and reliable, complete information. No warranties of any kind are declared or implied. Readers acknowledge that the author is not engaging in the rendering of legal, financial, medical or professional advice. The content within this book has been derived from various sources. Please consult a licensed professional before attempting any techniques outlined in this book.

By reading this document, the reader agrees that under no circumstances is the author responsible for any losses, direct or indirect, which are incurred as a result of the use of the information contained within this document, including, but not limited to, — errors, omissions, or inaccuracies.

Contents

Introduction

"The only constant in life is change" Heraclitus

As an equestrian coach, I had spent countless hours teaching others how to connect with horses. These powerful, magnificent creatures can partner with us and form a strong bond. It is not always about riding or technique but about understanding connections on a deeper level. I realized that how we build trust and communicate with horses mirrors many ways we should approach our human relationships. This revelation was a turning point for me as I reflected on my relationships and set me on a path to understanding what makes relationships thrive.

As a best-selling author and licensed equestrian coach, I've dedicated my life to helping individuals achieve success. With my background in sales, life coaching, equestrian coaching and women's leadership skills, I have guided many on their journey to reach their dreams and goals. My commitment is to empower and inspire those who wish to improve their connections with others.

This book offers practical steps to break free from toxic patterns and establish healthy boundaries. You will find strategies to enhance communication, improve listening skills, and build emotional intimacy. The aim is to provide actionable advice and real-life examples that you can apply in your relationships.

The book's structure is simple yet effective. Each chapter addresses a specific aspect of healthy relationships. You will find practical applications, relatable examples, and valuable resources. This organization will help you quickly find key points and apply the insights to your life.

Why are healthy relationships so essential and meaningful? They are the foundation of personal well-being and overall life satisfaction. Research shows that people with strong, supportive relationships live longer and experience less stress. Investing in your relationships can lead to a happier and more fulfilling life.

Yet, we all face challenges. Many adults struggle with communication breakdowns, trust issues, and emotional disconnect, which can lead to conflict and dissatisfaction. This book addresses these issues head-on, offering solutions and strategies to help you navigate them.

What can you expect from venturing down this path? You will learn practical techniques to improve your relationships. This book covers everything from effective communication and conflict resolution to setting boundaries and building emotional intimacy. Engage with the content and apply the exercises. You'll find that small changes can lead to significant improvements. Keep a notebook handy to write down any key take aways and important content that applies to you.

Approach this book with a growth mindset. Be open to change. Self-awareness and personal development are vital to achieving healthy relationships. Be patient with yourself. Growth takes time and effort, but the rewards are worth it!

Applying the teachings of this book can yield positive outcomes. Imagine better communication with your partner, deeper emotional connections with friends, family, and more effective conflict resolution with colleagues or your partner. Your overall relationship satisfaction will improve, enriching your life in countless ways.

As we begin this journey together, I encourage you to embrace the transformative power of self-discovery and personal growth. Take the first step towards more substantial and fulfilling connections. The path to healthy relationships can be challenging but worth taking. Welcome to a world where your relationships can thrive and you can find joy and satisfaction in your connections with others. I hope this book inspires you to create deeper, more meaningful connections in every area of your life—with family, friends, colleagues, and your partner.

Chapter I

Understanding the Foundation of Healthy Relationships

Have you ever wondered why some relationships thrive while others struggle constantly? It's a question I found myself asking years ago while navigating the complexities of my relationships. The turning point came during a particularly challenging period in my life. I have always dedicated my career as an equestrian coach, but some of my connections with my partner started to test me. One evening, after a weekend of coaching at a national show qualifier, I argued with my spouse about time commitments spent at horse shows. We never went over our schedules or discussed how much time was required. I realized that the principles I used to build trust with horses—consistency, clear communication, and mutual respect—were the same principles I struggled with in my relationships. This insight made me realize I needed to change how I approached every relationship. Let me share how I turned my coaching skills to inspire others to connect with others and cultivate healthy relationships.

1.1 Defining a Healthy Relationship

Healthy relationships are built on a foundation of mutual respect and admiration. This means valuing each other as equals, acknowledging each other's strengths, and supporting each other's growth. Mutual respect fosters an environment where both partners feel valued and appreciated. It's about seeing your partner as a whole person and recognizing their contributions to the relationship. Without this respect, the relationship can become unbalanced, leading to resentment and conflict.

Trust and reliability are also cornerstones of healthy relationships. Trust is the confidence that your partner will act in your best interest and be there for you when needed. Reliability means consistently showing up and following through on promises. When trust and reliability are present, partners can feel secure and supported, knowing they can rely on each other in times of need. Trust isn't just about fidelity; it's about knowing that your partner has your back and will support you through thick and thin.

Effective and open communication is another critical element. It involves more than just talking; it's about listening, understanding, and responding appropriately. Open communication means being honest about your feelings and needs and being receptive to your partner's. It's about creating a safe space where both partners can express themselves without fear of judgment or retaliation. Effective communication helps prevent misunderstandings and resolves conflicts before they escalate.

Shared values and goals are essential for long-term compatibility. Partners with similar values and aspirations are likelier to work together towards common objectives. This alignment can include everything from how you handle finances to your views on family and career ambitions. When partners are on the same page, it's easier to navigate life's challenges together and make decisions that support the relationship's growth.

Emotional intimacy is vital for fostering a deep connection between partners. This involves being emotionally vulnerable, sharing personal thoughts and feelings, and providing consistent emotional support. Emotional intimacy creates a bond that goes beyond the physical aspect of the relationship. It's about feeling understood and accepted for who you are. When partners are emotionally intimate, they can weather life's storms together and become stronger on the other side.

Physical intimacy complements emotional intimacy but is not the sole determinant of a healthy relationship. Physical intimacy includes affectionate gestures like hugs and kisses, as well as sexual compatibility. These physical expressions of love and affection help to reinforce the emotional connection. However, a relationship that relies solely on physical intimacy without emotional depth may struggle to endure over time.

Consider the case of Jane and Mark, a couple who faced significant challenges early in their relationship. Jane felt that Mark wasn't listening to her, while Mark believed Jane didn't trust him. They decided to work on their communication skills by setting aside time each day to talk openly about their feelings and concerns. They learned to trust each other more through consistent effort and built a stronger emotional connection. Their relationship transformed from one filled with misunderstandings to a partnership based on mutual respect, trust, and open communication.

Relationship experts agree that healthy relationships are about balance and mutual effort. As Dr. John Gottman, a renowned relationship researcher, states, "The successful couples are the ones who can repair the relationship after a conflict, not the ones who avoid conflict altogether." This advice underscores the importance of communication and emotional intimacy in maintaining a healthy relationship.

Healthy relationships are multifaceted, requiring mutual respect, trust, effective communication, shared values, and emotional and physical intimacy. Each element supports the others, creating a balanced and fulfilling partnership. Through real-life examples and expert insights, it becomes clear that building and maintaining a healthy relationship is an ongoing process that requires effort and commitment from both partners.

1.2 The Role of Self-Awareness in Relationships

Self-awareness is the ability to recognize and understand your own emotions, thoughts, and behaviors. It's about knowing what makes you tick, what triggers your reactions, and how your actions affect those around you. In the context of relationships, self-awareness is crucial. It allows you to understand your emotional landscape, which in turn helps you navigate interactions with your partner more effectively. When you know yourself well, you can clearly communicate your needs and desires, reducing misunderstandings and conflicts. This understanding lays the groundwork for a healthier, more harmonious relationship.

One of the significant benefits of self-awareness is improved emotional regulation. By understanding your emotional triggers, you can better manage your reactions. For example, if you know you tend to get irritable when you're hungry, you can avoid conflicts by ensuring you eat regularly. This might seem simple, but it can profoundly impact your relationship. When both partners are aware of their triggers and manage their emotions effectively, it leads to a more stable and peaceful relationship environment. This emotional stability allows for deeper connections and more meaningful interactions.

Enhanced empathy is another benefit of self-awareness. When you understand your own emotions and behaviors, you become more attuned to the feelings and behaviors of others. Heightened empathy allows you to respond to your partner's needs more effectively. For instance, if your partner is upset, self-awareness can help you recognize their distress and offer support rather than reacting defensively. This empathy fosters a deeper emotional connection and builds trust, making your relationship more resilient to challenges. Understanding each other on this level can transform how you interact and resolve conflicts.

There are several practical techniques for increasing self-awareness. Mindfulness practices, such as meditation and deep breathing exercises, can help you stay present and observe your thoughts and emotions without judgment. This practice allows you to become more aware of your internal state and how it affects your behavior. Journaling exercises are another powerful tool. You can gain insights into your emotional patterns and triggers by writing down your thoughts and feelings. Regular self-reflection, whether through journaling or quiet contemplation, helps you understand the underlying causes of your emotions and behaviors.

Let's consider a real-life scenario to illustrate the impact of self-awareness. Imagine a couple, Sarah and John, who frequently argue about household chores. Sarah feels overwhelmed and unappreciated, while John feels nagged and unrecognized for his efforts. Through self-awareness, Sarah realizes her frustration stems from a more profound feeling of unsupported. On the other hand, John recognizes that his defensiveness arises from a fear of failure. By understanding these underlying emotions, they can communicate more effectively. Sarah can express her need for support without accusing John, and John can acknowledge his insecurities and work on them. This self-awareness helps them navigate their conflicts more constructively.

Personal growth stories further highlight the importance of self-awareness. Take, for example, a woman who struggled with jealousy in her relationships. Through self-awareness practices, she discovered that her jealousy was rooted in past experiences of betrayal. By recognizing this, she could communicate her insecurities to her partner and work on building trust. This improved her current relationship and helped her heal from past wounds. Her story shows how self-awareness can lead to significant personal and relational growth.

The role of self-awareness in relationships cannot emphasized. It is the foundation upon which healthy, fulfilling relationships are built. Understanding your emotions and behaviors allows you to navigate your interactions more emotionally and with greater empathy. Whether through mindfulness, journaling, or self-reflection, increasing your self-awareness is a decisive step toward improving your relationship dynamics. The profound benefits lead to more meaningful connections, fewer conflicts, and a deeper understanding of yourself and your partner.

1.3 Identifying and Expressing Feelings

Understanding and articulating our feelings should be considered, as they are often overlooked. Yet, it's a fundamental step in effective communication—many drift through conversations without genuinely tapping into what we feel, leading to miscommunication and unresolved conflicts. Differentiating between primary emotions, such as sadness, anger, or joy, and secondary emotions, like frustration or jealousy, is crucial. Primary emotions are the raw, initial reactions we experience, while secondary emotions often mask or layer over these initial feelings, complicating our understanding. Recognizing these layers helps address the root of our emotions, allowing us to communicate more clearly and effectively. Emotional triggers, those stimuli that provoke intense emotional reactions, also play a significant role in how we express ourselves. Knowing what sets off these reactions enables us to manage them better, leading to healthier interactions.

Several practical methods can be employed to become more adept at recognizing emotions. Emotional check-ins are a simple yet effective practice. Take a moment each day to pause and ask yourself, "What am I feeling right now?" This practice fosters a habit of self-reflection and awareness. Emotion wheels can be a helpful visual tool. They display a range of emotions, allowing you to pinpoint your feelings, which can be beneficial when emotions are complex or overwhelming. Writing down your thoughts and feelings with reflection exercises can also be helpful. Putting pen to paper creates a tangible record of your emotional state, providing insights into patterns and triggers. When practiced regularly, these methods enhance your ability to identify and understand your emotions, paving the way for more meaningful communication.

Once you have identified your emotions, effectively expressing them is the next step. Using "I" statements is a powerful technique. Instead of saying, "You never listen to me," try, "I feel unheard when I'm interrupted." This approach focuses on your feelings rather than placing blame, reducing defensiveness and opening the door to constructive dialogue. Avoiding blame language is equally important. Phrases like "You make me so angry" can escalate tensions. Instead, focus on expressing how specific actions affect you personally. This shift in language fosters a more supportive and understanding environment where both partners feel safe to share their emotions without fear of conflict.

Practical examples can illustrate these concepts effectively. Imagine a scenario where a couple faces a disagreement about household chores. Instead of accusing one another, they use "I" statements to convey their feelings. One partner might say, "I feel overwhelmed when I see dishes piling up," prompting the other to respond with understanding rather than defensiveness. Another example could involve expressing frustration at work. Instead of venting angrily, you might tell a colleague, "I feel stressed when deadlines overlap, and it's challenging to manage everything." This clarity of expression allows for a more productive conversation focused on finding solutions rather than assigning blame.

Successful emotional communication can transform relationships. Consider a couple dealing with a recurring issue of spending too much time on their phones during dinner. They decide to express their feelings using the techniques discussed. One might say, "I feel disconnected when we don't talk during dinner," while the other responds, "I didn't realize it made you feel that way; let's set our phones aside." This exchange, rooted in understanding and clear expression, strengthens their connection and leads to a mutually agreeable solution. By identifying and expressing feelings with clarity and compassion, we create an environment where honest communication thrives, misunderstandings diminish, and relationships flourish.

1.4 Emotional Intelligence and Its Impact on Relationships

Emotional intelligence, often abbreviated as EQ, is a crucial factor in the health and stability of relationships. At its core, EQ encompasses four main components: self-awareness, self-regulation, social awareness, and relationship management. Self-awareness involves recognizing and understanding our own emotions. It's about being in tune with what we feel and why. Self-regulation is the ability to manage those emotions, ensuring they don't dictate our actions in a harmful way. Social awareness pertains to our capacity to empathize with others and understand their feelings and perspectives. Lastly, relationship management maintains healthy interactions, resolves conflicts, and fosters positive connections. Together, these components create a framework for understanding and navigating the complex landscape of human emotions.

The importance of emotional intelligence in relationships cannot be overstated. A high level of EQ enhances empathy, allowing us to connect with our partners on a deeper emotional level. When we can empathize, we understand our partner's feelings and can respond with compassion and support. This empathy fosters a sense of trust and safety, which is essential for any healthy relationship. Furthermore, EQ plays a pivotal role in conflict resolution. Instead of reacting impulsively during disagreements, emotionally intelligent individuals can pause, assess their emotions, and respond thoughtfully. This ability to manage emotions reduces the likelihood of escalating conflicts and promotes constructive dialogue. Stronger emotional connections are another significant benefit. Partners with high EQ can communicate more openly and honestly, creating a bond built on mutual understanding and respect. This emotional connection serves as the foundation for a lasting relationship.

Improving emotional intelligence is a journey that requires intentional effort and practice. Empathy-building exercises are an excellent starting point. One effective exercise is regularly engaging in active listening, focusing entirely on your partner without interrupting. This practice not only improves empathy but also strengthens your connection. Emotional regulation strategies are equally important. Techniques such as deep breathing, mindfulness, and cognitive reframing can help manage intense emotions, preventing them from harming your relationship. For instance, when feeling overwhelmed, taking a few deep breaths can help calm your mind, allowing you to respond more rationally. Regular self-reflection can also enhance EQ. Setting aside time to reflect on your interactions, considering what went well and what could be improved, fosters continuous growth. Integrating these practices into your daily life can gradually increase your emotional intelligence, benefiting yourself and your relationships.

Research supports the profound impact of emotional intelligence on relationship satisfaction. Studies have shown that couples with high EQ experience greater marital satisfaction, better communication, and fewer conflicts. For example, a study published in the Journal of Marriage and Family found that couples with high emotional intelligence better manage stress and resolve conflicts, leading to more harmonious relationships. These findings underscore the importance of developing EQ for relationship health.

Consider the case of Emily and James, a couple who struggled with frequent arguments and misunderstandings. They decided to work on their emotional intelligence by practicing empathy and improving their communication skills. Emily began actively listening to James, trying to understand his perspective without interrupting. James, in turn, focused on managing his emotions, using deep breathing techniques to stay calm during heated discussions. Over time, their efforts paid off. They found that their conflicts became less frequent and more manageable. They could communicate more openly and honestly, strengthening their emotional connection. Their relationship transformed from one fraught with tension to a partnership characterized by mutual respect and understanding.

As we conclude this section, emotional intelligence is a powerful tool for enhancing relationships. By cultivating self-awareness, self-regulation, social awareness, and relationship management, we can navigate our emotions more effectively and build stronger, more fulfilling connections. Improving EQ may require effort and dedication, but the rewards are worth it. By fostering emotional intelligence, we enhance our relationships and enrich our emotional well-being, leading to a more harmonious and satisfying life.

Chapter 2

Navigating Different Personalities

Enneagram Types

Have you ever felt like you were speaking a different language than your partner, friend, or colleague? It's a shared experience I've encountered frequently in my personal and professional life. I remember a time when I was participating with a diverse group of women in a leadership workshop. Each participant had a unique way of approaching problems, and what worked for one person didn't necessarily resonate with another. During this workshop, I first discovered the Enneagram as a tool for understanding these differences. The response was overwhelmingly positive as participants began to see their interactions in a new light as they applied this tool, recognizing the distinct personality types that shaped their behaviors and relationships.

The Enneagram is a personality system that offers profound insights into human behavior and relationships. It categorizes personalities into nine distinct types, each with characteristics, motivations, and fears. This system provides a framework for understanding oneself and how different personalities interact. Historically, the Enneagram has roots in ancient spiritual traditions but was popularized in the 20th century by psychologists and spiritual teachers. Its relevance to personal growth and relationships lies in its ability to illuminate the unconscious patterns that drive our actions. By identifying your Enneagram type, you gain self-awareness and a deeper understanding of how you relate to others. This understanding can lead to more compassionate and effective interactions.

Let's explore each of the nine Enneagram types in detail.

1. The Reformer, is characterized by a conscientious, purposeful nature. They always strive for improvement and perfection. They value integrity and often have a strong sense of right and wrong.

2. The Helper, is caring and interpersonal, driven by a desire to be loved and appreciated. They are generous and empathetic but may struggle with boundaries.

3. The Achiever, is success-oriented and adaptable. They are motivated by the need to be valued and admired for their accomplishments. They are often energetic and goal-driven.

4. The Individualist, is sensitive and expressive. They seek to discover their identity and express their uniqueness. They are often creative but may feel misunderstood.

5. The Investigator, is perceptive and innovative, craving knowledge and understanding. They are observant and independent but can be detached.

6. The Loyalist, is committed and security-oriented, seeking safety and support. They are responsible and trustworthy but may be anxious.

7. The Enthusiast, is spontaneous and versatile. They seek new experiences and avoid pain. They are fun-loving and optimistic but may struggle with focus.

8. The Challenger, is confident and decisive, valuing strength and

control. They are assertive and protective but can be confronta-
tional.

9. The Peacemaker, is easygoing and accommodating. They seek
harmony and peace. They are accepting and supportive but may
avoid conflict.

Understanding the interactions between these types can enrich your relationships. For example, a Type 1 and Type 7 pairing might experience tension due to their differing approaches to life—one seeking structure, the other spontaneity. However, they can complement each other by balancing each other's tendencies. Similarly, a Type 3 and Type 9 dynamic might involve one partner driving for success while the other prefers harmony, leading to potential misunderstandings and growth opportunities. Each Enneagram pairing has unique dynamics that can either enhance or challenge the relationship.

To apply Enneagram insights practically, consider tailoring your communication strategies to suit different types. For instance, when interacting with a Type 5, provide space and time for reflection, while a Type 2 might appreciate personal gestures of appreciation. Understanding these personality differences can guide more empathetic and effective interactions in conflict resolution. The Enneagram strategy can help plan activities that align with each type's preferences, creating more harmonious and fulfilling relationships. Understanding and applying the Enneagram can transform your relationships by fostering deeper connections and mutual respect.

2.2 Managing Introvert-Extrovert Dynamics

Understanding the dynamics of introversion and extroversion can be a game-changer in any relationship. Introverts typically draw energy from within, finding solace in solitude and quiet reflection. They often prefer smaller, more intimate gatherings where deep conversations can flourish. In contrast, extroverts are energized by external stimuli, thriving in social settings and frequently seeking out the buzz of a lively environment. They relish interaction and often feel invigorated after engaging with others. These core differences affect how introverts and extroverts communicate and interact. Introverts may prefer written communication or one-on-one conversations, taking time to process their thoughts before speaking. Extroverts, on the other hand, tend to think out loud, processing information through dialogue and group discussions. These differing preferences can lead to misunderstandings if not acknowledged and respected.

Balancing these differences presents challenges, but they are manageable. One common issue is finding the right balance between social activities and alone time. Extroverts prefer little downtime, while introverts can become overwhelmed if social demands are too high. This tension can lead to conflict, especially when one partner feels that their needs are neglected. Another challenge is navigating communication differences. An introvert might perceive an extrovert's enthusiasm as overwhelming, while the extrovert might misinterpret the introvert's need for space as disinterest. A typical example is one partner wanting to attend a social event while the other prefers a quiet night at home. This can create friction if both partners don't communicate their needs effectively.

Compromise here is crucial. Partners can agree to alternate between social outings and quieter activities, ensuring both their needs are met. Scheduling regular quiet time for introverts can provide the space they need to recharge while planning social outings for extroverts, which allows them to fulfill their need for interaction. Open communication is critical, with both partners expressing their preferences and finding a middle ground. For instance, an introvert might agree to attend a party with an extrovert with the understanding that they'll leave after a couple of hours. In return, the extrovert might agree to spend the following evening at home, enjoying a quiet dinner together. This mutual respect addresses each other's needs, can prevent misunderstandings, and strengthens the relationship.

Real-life examples highlight the success of these strategies. Consider a couple, Alex and Jamie, who initially struggled with their different social preferences. Alex, an extrovert, loved hosting gatherings and attending social events, while Jamie, an introvert, preferred quiet evenings and small group interactions. They found a balance that worked for both by openly discussing their needs. They decided on a schedule that included social outings and downtime, allowing each to recharge in their preferred way. Alex discovered the joy of quieter activities, while Jamie learned to appreciate the energy of larger gatherings. Their mutual understanding deepened their connection, leading to a more harmonious relationship. A testimonial from Jamie sums it up: "Respecting each other's social needs has brought us closer. We've learned to appreciate our differences, which has enriched our time together."

2.3 Attachment Styles Explained

In understanding how we connect with others, attachment theory offers valuable insights. Pioneered by John Bowlby and later expanded by Mary Ainsworth, this theory delves into the bonds formed in early childhood and their lasting impact on relationships. Bowlby described attachment as a "lasting psychological connectedness between human beings," emphasizing its role in survival by keeping children close to caregivers. Ainsworth built upon this with her "strange situation" study, identifying distinct attachment styles that affect behaviors throughout life. These early bonds shape how we relate to caregivers and interact in adult relationships, influencing everything from communication patterns to emotional needs.

Attachment styles fall into four primary categories. Secure attachment is often the most stable, marked by comfort with intimacy and independence. Individuals with this style find it easy to connect while maintaining their autonomy. Anxious attachment, on the other hand, involves a preoccupation with relationships and a fear of abandonment. These individuals often seek reassurance and may worry about their partner's commitment. Avoidant attachment is characterized by discomfort with closeness and a reliance on self-sufficiency. Such individuals may prioritize independence over intimacy, often withdrawing during conflicts. Finally, disorganized attachment combines elements of both anxious and avoidant styles, leading to inconsistent behaviors and confusion about relationships. This style can stem from unpredictable caregiving in childhood, resulting in a need for more coherent strategies for dealing with relationships.

The impact of these attachment styles on relationships is profound. Securely attached individuals tend to communicate openly and resolve conflicts constructively. Their relationships often have mutual support and understanding. Anxiously attached individuals may struggle with communication, usually expressing their needs in a heightened emotional way, leading to misunderstandings. Conflicts can escalate as they seek constant reassurance. Avoidant individuals might avoid discussing issues altogether, retreating into themselves when faced with conflict, which can leave their partners feeling neglected. Disorganized attachment can lead to erratic behavior, where one's responses are unpredictable, creating an unstable relationship environment. For instance, a securely attached person might calmly express their feelings in a conflict. In contrast, an anxiously attached partner might react with heightened anxiety, seeking immediate resolution, and avoidant individuals might shut down, avoiding the conversation entirely.

Navigating these attachment styles requires understanding and intentional action. Enhancing secure attachment behaviors can involve fostering open communication and expressing needs clearly. It's about building trust and ensuring both partners feel valued. For those with anxious or avoidant tendencies, awareness is vital. Anxious individuals can benefit from reassurance and creating a safe, supportive environment where they feel secure. Avoidant individuals might work on opening up more gradually, sharing their thoughts and emotions in a safe space. For example, setting aside time for regular check-ins can help both partners express their feelings and concerns, reducing anxiety and promoting a sense of security. Encouraging honest dialogue, where each partner feels heard and respected, can bridge the gaps created by differing attachment styles. Relationships can flourish through understanding and adapting to these styles, allowing for deeper connections and emotional intimacy.

2.4 Avoidant and Anxious Attachment in Relationships

Understanding avoidant attachment begins with recognizing a deep-seated discomfort with intimacy. Individuals with this attachment style often prioritize independence and value self-sufficiency. This preference can manifest in relationships as a tendency to emotionally withdraw, especially during conflicts. It's not uncommon for avoidant partners to shut down or become distant when tensions rise, as they find it challenging to process emotions in the heat of the moment. For example, during a disagreement, an avoidant partner might retreat into silence, leaving their partner feeling isolated and unsure of how to proceed. This behavior stems from a protective mechanism developed over time, often rooted in past experiences where reliance on others felt risky or unfulfilling.

Anxious attachment is characterized by a persistent fear of abandonment and a strong need for reassurance. Individuals with this style are often highly attuned to their partner's emotional state, sometimes to the point of heightened sensitivity. This can lead to a constant need for validation and a preoccupation with the relationship's status. Anxious partners may frequently seek affirmation of their partner's love and commitment, fearing that any sign of distance could signal impending separation. For instance, if a partner is less communicative one day, an anxious individual might worry excessively about what it means, seeking constant contact to alleviate their insecurities. This need for reassurance can strain the relationship, as their partner may perceive it as clinginess or insecurity.

Balancing these contrasting behaviors requires intentional strategies and mutual understanding. Open and honest communication is vital in navigating the complexities of avoidant and anxious dynamics. Encouraging discussions about feelings and needs can help bridge gaps and foster a sense of security. Building trust involves creating a safe environment where both partners feel heard and valued. For instance, setting regular times to discuss relationship concerns can provide a structured space for sharing and reassurance. This practice addresses immediate issues and reinforces the relationship's foundation, allowing both partners to feel secure and understood.

Real-life success stories can offer valuable insights into managing these dynamics. Consider the story of Jake and Emily, who faced significant challenges due to their differing attachment styles. With an avoidant attachment, Jake often withdrew during conflicts, leaving Emily, who had an anxious attachment, feeling unsupported and anxious. Recognizing the pattern, they committed to regular "communication evenings" where they could express their thoughts and feelings without interruption. Over time, Jake learned to articulate his need for space without shutting down while Emily practiced patience and self-soothing techniques. Their relationship flourished as they each tried to understand and accommodate the other's needs. Emily reflected on their progress: "Understanding our attachment styles, we've learned to respect our differences, which has made us stronger as a couple."

This chapter has explored the intricate dynamics of avoidant and anxious attachment in relationships. Understanding these patterns allows you to navigate your relationships more effectively, fostering stronger connections and emotional resilience.

Chapter 3

———————————

Emotional Intelligence and Self-Awareness

Picture this: you're in the middle of a bustling café, the chatter around you a comforting hum. A couple at the nearby table catches your eye; they're leaning in, speaking softly, and you can almost feel their connection. Suddenly, the energy shifts. One of them raises their voice, and frustration is evident. Yet, instead of escalating, the other takes a deep breath, listens intently, and responds with calm empathy. This scene, familiar to many of us, highlights a crucial skill—emotional intelligence, or EQ. Defined as the ability to perceive, process, and regulate emotions in oneself and others, EQ encompasses self-awareness, self-regulation, motivation, empathy, and social skills. These components are the building blocks of navigating the complex tapestry of human emotions and interactions.

Self-awareness is the cornerstone of emotional intelligence. It involves understanding your own emotions, strengths, and weaknesses. This awareness allows you to recognize how your feelings affect your behavior and relationships. Self-regulation follows, empowering you to manage your emotions effectively. This means not allowing anger, anxiety, or sadness to dictate your actions. Motivation, another critical element, is the drive to pursue goals with energy and persistence. It's about harnessing emotions to fuel your ambitions. Empathy, the ability to understand and share the feelings of others, bridges the gap between people, fostering more profound connections. Lastly, social skills, the tools for managing relationships, are essential for effective communication and conflict resolution. Together, these elements create a framework for understanding and navigating the emotional landscape of relationships.

High emotional intelligence can transform your relationships and personal well-being. It enhances communication by helping you express yourself clearly and listen empathetically. This skill is invaluable in resolving conflicts, allowing you to approach disagreements with calmness and understanding. Stronger emotional connections result from empathy and social skills, leading to more fulfilling relationships. Moreover, EQ aids in managing stress, equipping you with tools to remain composed in challenging situations. It fosters enhanced empathy, enabling you to see situations from others' perspectives and respond compassionately. These benefits contribute to a more harmonious and satisfying life, underscoring the profound impact of emotional intelligence.

Unlike cognitive intelligence, or IQ, which measures analytical and problem-solving abilities, EQ focuses on emotional and social complexities. IQ is relatively fixed, providing a baseline for cognitive tasks, but EQ can be developed over time, offering opportunities for growth and improvement. While IQ helps you solve mathematical problems, EQ guides you in handling interpersonal challenges. The balance between these intelligences is crucial for overall success and happiness. EQ often proves more impactful than IQ in professions requiring collaboration and leadership. The ability to connect with others, manage emotions, and navigate social situations usually determines success in both personal and professional spheres.

Consider a real-life scenario: a person recognizes their rising anger during a heated argument. Instead of reacting impulsively, they pause, take a deep breath, and respond thoughtfully, de-escalating the situation. This scenario exemplifies emotional intelligence in action, demonstrating self-regulation and empathy. In another instance, using empathy to comfort a grieving friend shows the power of understanding and shared emotion. A leader employing EQ to motivate their team creates an environment of trust and collaboration, fostering productivity and morale. These examples illustrate the tangible benefits of emotional intelligence, offering a blueprint for enhancing your interactions and relationships.

Interactive Exercise: Identifying Your EQ Strengths

Spend a few minutes reflecting on situations where you effectively managed your emotions or empathized with others. Consider what you did well and what you might improve. Write down your thoughts, focusing on how you can apply these insights to enhance your emotional intelligence. This exercise will help you identify and develop your EQ strengths, contributing to more fulfilling relationships and personal growth.

3.2 Developing Self-Awareness

Self-awareness is the foundation upon which emotional intelligence is built. It empowers you to understand your emotions and recognize their influence on your behavior. Without self-awareness, emotions can feel uncontrollable, dictating your reactions and decisions. When you know your emotional landscape, you can step back and assess situations more objectively. This perspective helps you communicate more effectively and prevents misunderstandings. Imagine you're stressed at work and snap at a colleague. Self-awareness allows you to recognize stress as the root cause, helping you address it rather than misdirecting your frustration. Recognizing how emotions influence behavior is crucial in breaking patterns that might lead to conflict or discontent. Through this understanding, you can cultivate more meaningful connections with others as you become attuned to your needs and those around you.

Techniques to increase self-awareness are varied and can be tailored to suit your preferences. Mindfulness meditation is a powerful tool encouraging you to observe your thoughts and emotions without judgment. By practicing mindfulness, you become more present and aware of your inner experiences, which cultivates a deeper understanding of your emotional responses. Keeping an emotions journal is another effective method. Taking a few minutes each day to reflect on your emotional experiences can provide valuable insights into your patterns and triggers. This practice enhances self-awareness and offers a sense of clarity and perspective. For instance, if you notice a recurring theme of anxiety in your journal, you can explore the underlying causes and seek ways to address them. Daily reflection on your emotions fosters a greater understanding of yourself and equips you to navigate your relationships with authenticity and empathy.

Feedback from others plays a pivotal role in developing self-awareness. Those close to us can often offer insights into our behaviors that we might not readily see. Seeking feedback from trusted friends or partners can provide a fresh perspective on how you interact with others. When you receive feedback, take the time to reflect on it and consider how it aligns with your self-perception. This process can lead to profound self-discovery and growth. For example, a partner might point out that you tend to withdraw during disagreements, prompting you to explore the reasons behind this behavior. Acknowledging and addressing these patterns can foster healthier communication and connection. Feedback is a gift that allows you to expand your self-awareness and improve your interactions with others.

Real-life examples of individuals who have developed self-awareness highlight its transformative impact on relationships. Take Sarah, who struggled with feelings of inadequacy in her marriage. Through mindfulness meditation and journaling, she identified her tendency to self-criticize and realized how it affected her interactions with her spouse. By seeking feedback from her partner, she gained further insights into her behavior and worked to cultivate self-compassion. As Sarah's self-awareness grew, so did her ability to communicate openly and vulnerably, strengthening her relationship. Another testimonial comes from James, who regularly engaged in self-reflection. His increased self-awareness allowed him to recognize when he was projecting his stress onto his family, enabling him to take responsibility and seek healthier ways to cope. James's commitment to self-awareness improved his relationships and enhanced his overall well-being. These stories illustrate the profound impact that self-awareness can have on personal growth and the quality of our connections.

3.3 Managing Emotions Effectively

Emotions, when left unchecked, can stir up chaos in our lives. Imagine a day that starts peacefully but quickly turns tumultuous because of a simple misunderstanding. You find yourself reacting with irritation, and before you know it, a minor issue escalates into a full-blown argument. Emotional regulation serves as the anchor that prevents such storms. It is crucial for maintaining healthy relationships and personal well-being. By managing our emotions, we can avoid outbursts that might otherwise damage our bonds with others. This control reduces stress and anxiety and enhances our ability to solve problems effectively. When we are not overwhelmed by our emotions, we can think more clearly and make better decisions in personal and professional settings.

Fortunately, there are practical methods for keeping our emotions in check. Deep breathing exercises are a simple yet powerful tool. By focusing on your breath, inhaling slowly, and exhaling deeply, you can calm your nervous system and regain control over your emotional state. Progressive muscle relaxation is another technique that involves tensing and slowly releasing each muscle group in your body, helping relieve physical tension and mental stress. Cognitive restructuring, or challenging negative thoughts, is equally compelling. It involves identifying irrational or unhelpful thoughts and replacing them with more balanced and constructive perspectives. This shift in thinking can transform how you perceive and respond to challenging situations.

Mindfulness practices are invaluable in emotion regulation. Mindfulness meditation, for instance, encourages you to observe your thoughts and feelings without judgment. This practice allows you to become more aware of your emotional triggers and responses, giving you the power to change them. , the sensation of your feet touching the ground; grounding techniques can help you stay present during stressful moments. Sensory awareness exercises, such as paying attention to the sights, sounds, and smells around you, promote a sense of calm and clarity, helping to manage emotions and enhance overall mindfulness, leading to greater emotional stability.

Consider a scenario where you find yourself in a heated argument with a loved one. Instead of letting anger take over, you pause, take a deep breath, and let the tension dissipate. This simple act can defuse the situation and pave the way for a more constructive conversation. Practicing mindfulness helps you stay grounded during such moments, enabling you to respond with thoughtfulness rather than react impulsively. Reframing negative thoughts is another powerful strategy. When faced with a stressful situation, instead of thinking, "This is unbearable," you might say, "This is challenging, but I can handle it." This shift in perspective reduces emotional distress and empowers you to tackle problems with resilience.

Exercise: Practicing Mindfulness to Stay Present

Take five minutes each day to practice mindfulness. Sit quietly, close your eyes, and focus on your breath. Notice each inhale and exhale. Whenever your mind wanders, gently bring your focus back to your breath. This exercise helps you cultivate mindfulness, making it easier to manage emotions in stressful situations. Incorporating these practices into your daily routine will better prepare you to handle life's emotional highs and lows with grace and composure.

3.4 The Role of Empathy in Relationships

Empathy is the ability to understand and share the feelings of another, and it comes in several forms. Cognitive empathy involves seeing the world through someone else's eyes and understanding their perspective without feeling emotions. It's about mentally stepping into another person's shoes and recognizing their viewpoint. Emotional empathy allows you to feel what another person is experiencing, creating an emotional connection that lets you share in their joy and sorrow. Lastly, compassionate empathy goes beyond understanding and feeling. It compels you to take action to help, driven by the shared emotion. These forms of empathy work together to create a rich network of understanding and connection in relationships.

Empathy is transformative in relationships, enhancing trust and emotional intimacy. When you genuinely understand another's perspective and feelings, it builds a foundation of trust. This understanding acts as a bridge, connecting you to your partner, friend, or family member on a deeper level. Empathy also improves communication and conflict resolution. When you approach disagreements with empathy, you focus on understanding rather than defending, which paves the way for more constructive conversations. This empathetic approach fosters compassion and support, creating a safe space where both parties feel valued and heard. Empathy makes relationships more resilient, enabling you to navigate challenges with mutual respect and care.

Cultivating empathy requires intentional practice, but it is well worth the effort. Active listening is a powerful tool in this endeavor. When you listen with compassion, you focus entirely on the speaker, setting aside your judgments and responses. This involves being present and attentive, showing that you value what the other person is expressing. Perspective-taking exercises can further enhance your empathetic skills. Imagine yourself in the other person's situation, considering how they might feel and why. This practice broadens your understanding and deepens your connection. Empathy journaling is another effective method. By regularly reflecting on your interactions and emotions, you can develop greater awareness of your empathetic responses and identify areas for growth.

Practicing empathy can be woven into everyday life. Consider actively listening to a friend without jumping in with solutions. Instead, focus on genuinely understanding their feelings and validating their experiences.

This simple shift can affect how connected they feel to you. Another exercise is writing from the perspective of a partner or friend. Try to articulate their thoughts and emotions as if they were your own. This exercise can deepen your understanding and empathy for them. Engaging in volunteer work is a practical way to develop compassionate empathy. By helping those in need, you can experience the impact of empathetic action firsthand, reinforcing the importance of compassion in your relationships.

As we conclude this chapter, it is clear that empathy is a cornerstone of healthy, fulfilling relationships. It enhances communication, deepens emotional connections, and fosters a supportive environment. Empathy is not a fixed trait but a skill that can be nurtured and developed. Practicing empathy opens the door to more meaningful interactions and stronger bonds. The journey towards empathy is ongoing, with each moment offering an opportunity to connect more deeply with those around you. As you continue to explore these concepts, consider how empathy can transform your relationships and your understanding of yourself and others.

Chapter 4

Effective Communication Techniques

Imagine a dinner table where two people sit across each other, words flowing easily between them. Yet, one is scrolling through their phone, offering only intermittent nods and the occasional "uh-huh." The other person pauses, sensing a disconnect, their words falling into a void. This scenario is familiar to many, highlighting the importance of active listening in fostering genuine connection and understanding. Active listening is more than just hearing words; it's about engaging fully with the speaker's message, both spoken and unspoken. It requires undivided attention, allowing you to truly understand the intent behind the words. This skill is a cornerstone of effective communication and is vital for building trust and empathy in relationships. By mastering active listening, you can unlock the potential for deeper, more meaningful connections in your personal and professional life.

Active listening involves several key components, starting with focused attention. In a world filled with distractions, maintaining focus can be challenging. However, setting aside your phone, turning off the TV, and facing the speaker can create an environment conducive to meaningful dialogue. Paraphrasing and summarizing what the speaker has said are also crucial. By reflecting on their words, you demonstrate that you are hearing them and processing and understanding their message. This practice helps clarify misunderstandings and reinforces the speaker's feelings and thoughts. Avoiding interruptions is equally essential. Allowing the speaker to express themselves fully without interjecting fosters a sense of respect and validation, encouraging more open and honest communication.

To become a better listener, consider incorporating practical steps into your interactions. Nodding and offering verbal affirmations, such as "I see" or "That makes sense," can signal the speaker that you are engaged and interested in what they are saying. Asking open-ended questions is another powerful tool. These questions invite more than just a yes or no answer and encourage the speaker to expand on their thoughts and feelings. Reflective listening exercises can further enhance your skills. After the speaker has finished, take a moment to summarize their main points, asking if you've understood correctly. This practice ensures clarity and makes the speaker feel heard and valued.

Despite the benefits of active listening, several common barriers can impede our ability to listen effectively. Distractions, such as smartphones or background noise, can easily divert our attention from the speaker. Prejudgments, or preconceived notions about the speaker or topic, can also skew our perception and hinder genuine understanding. Emotional triggers, too, can disrupt listening. If a topic touches on a sensitive area, it may provoke a strong emotional reaction, making it challenging to remain objective and open. Recognizing these barriers is the first step in overcoming them. By consciously setting aside distractions and approaching conversations with an open mind, you can enhance your listening abilities and foster deeper connections.

Consider this real-life scenario: a partner attempts to share their feelings after a long day at work. The listener, distracted by their phone, offers only half-hearted responses. The partner, feeling unheard, becomes frustrated and withdraws. Contrast this with a situation where the listener sets aside distractions, maintains eye contact, and nods encouragingly. They ask, "Can you tell me more about how that made you feel?" This simple engagement transforms the interaction, allowing the partner to feel validated and supported. Through active listening, the listener creates an environment where open communication thrives, paving the way for stronger, more meaningful relationships.

Practice Exercise: Reflective Listening

Choose a quiet moment with a partner or friend to practice reflective listening. Ask them to share a recent experience, nod, and offer verbal affirmations as they speak. After they finish, paraphrase what they've said and ask if you've understood correctly. This exercise will help you refine your listening skills and enhance your ability to connect with others.

4.2 Using "I" Statements to Express Needs

Communication often fails when we focus on what others are doing wrong rather than expressing how their actions affect us. "I" statements come into play, emphasizing the importance of taking ownership of our feelings. By expressing your own experiences, "I" statements reduce defensiveness in the listener, fostering a more open and constructive dialogue. Instead of saying, "You never listen to me," which might put the other person on the defensive, using an "I" statement shifts the focus: "I feel unheard when I share my thoughts and don't get a response." This approach validates your emotions and creates a safe space for honest communication, inviting the other person to engage without feeling attacked. The power of 'I' statements lies in their ability to transform communication, empowering you to express your needs and feelings confidently and clearly.

The structure of an "I" statement is straightforward yet effective. It comprises three components: the emotion you feel, the specific situation prompting that emotion, and the reason behind it. For example, "I feel hurt when you interrupt me because it makes me feel unimportant." This formula ensures clarity, allowing the speaker to express their feelings and the listener to understand the impact of their actions. Practicing this structure can transform interactions, leading to more empathetic and productive conversations. By clearly stating the emotion, situation, and reason, you provide a complete picture, making it easier for others to respond with understanding and empathy. This clarity reduces misunderstandings and promotes healthier interactions.

To help you incorporate "I" statements into your communication, engage in practice exercises. Start with role-playing scenarios where you and a partner take turns expressing needs using "I" statements. This exercise allows you to explore different situations and refine your delivery. Writing exercises can also be beneficial. Take a moment to jot down a few "I" statements related to recent experiences, focusing on expressing your emotions clearly and honestly. This practice helps reinforce the structure and makes it easier to apply in real-life situations. Regularly practicing, you become more comfortable with this technique, enhancing your communication ability and building confidence in expressing your needs and feelings.

Real-life examples illustrate the profound impact of 'I' statements on communication. Consider a couple who frequently argued about household responsibilities. The arguments often escalated, leaving both partners feeling frustrated and unheard. By adopting 'I' statements, they reframed their discussions. One partner expressed, 'I feel overwhelmed when the house is messy because it adds to my stress.' This approach shifted their dynamic, allowing both to address the issue without blame. Another scenario could be a professional setting where a team struggles with a project. Instead of blaming each other, team members could use 'I' statements to express their concerns and needs, fostering a more open and constructive dialogue. Relationship counselors often commend 'I' statements for their ability to transform conflicts into opportunities for growth. Testimonials from practitioners highlight how this technique fosters empathy, understanding, and collaboration, essential elements for resolving disagreements constructively.

Incorporating "I" statements into your communication toolkit can significantly enhance relationships. By taking ownership of your emotions and expressing them clearly, you create an environment where open, honest dialogue can flourish. This approach reduces conflict and strengthens connections, paving the way for more meaningful and satisfying interactions. As you practice this technique, you will likely notice a shift in how others respond to you, leading to more productive and harmonious exchanges. Embrace the power of "I" statements and watch your relationships transform, becoming more resilient and fulfilling.

4.3 Nonverbal Communication Cues

Imagine sitting across from someone, listening to their words, yet you sense something is amiss while they are talking. Their arms are crossed tightly across their chest, and their eyes seem to dart around the room. Though their words are pleasant, their body tells a different story. This scenario underscores the importance of nonverbal communication, which can significantly impact how messages are received. Nonverbal cues, like body language, facial expressions, and tone of voice, often carry more weight than words. They provide context and depth to our interactions, offering clues about feelings and intentions. When words and nonverbal signals align, communication feels authentic and transparent. But when they clash, confusion often arises, leaving both parties feeling misunderstood. Learning to interpret these cues accurately enhances understanding and connection, allowing you to respond empathetically and effectively.

Reading nonverbal cues requires attentiveness and practice. Recognizing signs of discomfort or anger, such as clenched fists or a furrowed brow, can help you gauge the emotional state of the person you're interacting with. Understanding these signals enables you to respond appropriately by offering comfort or addressing concerns. Identifying genuine expression versus forced smiles is another skill worth honing. A genuine smile typically involves the whole face, with eyes crinkling at the corners, while a forced smile may not reach the eyes, signaling insincerity or discomfort. These subtle distinctions can reveal much about a person's true feelings, providing invaluable context in personal and professional interactions.

Using nonverbal cues effectively can significantly enhance your ability to convey messages. Maintaining eye contact, for instance, signals engagement and sincerity, helping to build trust and rapport. However, striking a balance is essential, as too much eye contact can feel intimidating. Using appropriate gestures can also reinforce your words, adding emphasis and clarity. Aligning facial expressions with verbal messages ensures consistency, reducing the risk of mixed signals. For example, delivering praise with a warm smile and open posture amplifies the positivity of your words, creating a more impactful interaction. When employed thoughtfully, these techniques can elevate your communication, making it more compelling and persuasive.

Consider a scenario where mismatched verbal and nonverbal cues lead to confusion. Imagine telling a friend, "I'm happy for you," while frowning and avoiding eye contact. The nonverbal signals suggest otherwise despite your words, leaving the friend puzzled and perhaps even hurt. In contrast, envision a situation where nonverbal cues enhance communication. During a heartfelt conversation, you maintain steady eye contact, nodding in agreement and mirroring your friend's expressions. These cues convey empathy and understanding, reinforcing your words and deepening the connection. Such examples illustrate nonverbal communication's profound impact, shaping how messages are perceived and relationships are structured.

Visual Element: Nonverbal Communication Chart

Create a simple chart illustrating familiar nonverbal cues and their meanings. Include examples such as folded arms (defensiveness or discomfort), leaning in (interest or engagement), and a relaxed posture (openness or confidence). This visual aid can be a quick reference, helping you interpret signals more accurately in your daily interactions. Integrating these insights into your communication can enhance your ability to connect with others, fostering more substantial, authentic relationships.

4.4 The Value of Apologies

In any relationship, the ability to apologize sincerely serves as a crucial lifeline. Apologies go beyond words; they are a powerful tool for mending rifts and rebuilding bridges. When you acknowledge a mistake, you open the door to healing and reestablishing trust. This process begins with recognizing that you've caused harm and taking responsibility for your intentional actions. By doing so, you validate the feelings of the person hurt, showing them that their emotions matter and that you are committed to making amends.

A sincere apology consists of several essential components:

- There must be an acknowledgment of wrongdoing. The first step is clearly stating what went wrong without making excuses or shifting blame.

- It would be best if you expressed genuine remorse for the impact of your actions. Following this, offering a way to repair the damage shows your commitment to rectifying the situation. This action reinforces your sincerity through a gesture or a behavior change.

- A promise to change future behavior solidifies your intent to prevent similar issues from arising again, ensuring the other person feels reassured and valued.

Here are a few examples of well-constructed apologies. In a situation where a misunderstanding has caused tension, a thoughtful apology might sound like, "I misunderstood your intentions in yesterday's conversation, and I regret any confusion that caused. Let's clarify things and move forward together." Another scenario involves a broken promise.

One might say, "I know I promised to be there for your presentation but didn't attend. I'm truly sorry for letting you down. I want to make it up to you and ensure it doesn't happen again." These examples highlight the core elements of acknowledging the mistake, expressing regret, and offering to repair the relationship, leading to a stronger connection.

Equally important is the ability to accept apologies with grace and understanding. When someone offers a sincere apology, expressing appreciation for their acknowledgment can help reinforce the positive communication dynamic. It might involve saying, "Thank you for recognizing how I felt. I appreciate your willingness to address it." The next step is to discuss how to move forward, focusing on solutions and growth rather than dwelling on past grievances. This approach encourages a constructive dialogue, paving the way for renewed trust and cooperation. By welcoming apologies and engaging in open discussions about the future, you foster an environment where both parties feel respected and heard, ultimately strengthening the bond.

In this chapter, we've explored the transformative power of apologies in relationships. Acknowledging mistakes, expressing regret, and committing to change can mend rifts and rebuild trust. By embracing these practices, you create a space for healing and growth, leading to more resilient and fulfilling connections. As we move forward, consider how these principles can enhance your interactions, paving the way for deeper understanding and connection. Transitioning to the next chapter, we'll delve into conflict resolution strategies, building on the foundation of effective communication to address challenges constructively and collaboratively.

Chapter 5

Conflict Resolution Strategies

Relationship conflicts can feel like sudden storms, appearing out of nowhere and disrupting the calm. One minute, everything seems fine, and the next, you're caught in a heated argument, unsure of how it escalated so quickly. But what if you could predict these storms and even prevent them? Like recognizing the clouds before a downpour, identifying conflict triggers in your relationships can help you navigate these turbulent moments more clearly and calmly. Understanding what sets off these conflicts—these triggers—is a crucial step in managing and resolving them effectively. Conflict triggers are the catalysts for disagreements, the underlying issues that prompt reactions and intensify emotions. They can be emotional, such as feeling disrespected, or situational, like financial stress. Recognizing these triggers is essential because it allows you to address the root cause of conflicts rather than just the symptoms.

Relationship triggers often include misunderstandings and miscommunications arising from assumptions or unclear expectations. When communication falters, it becomes easy to misinterpret intentions, leading to unnecessary disputes. Unmet expectations are another frequent source of conflict, especially when partners have unspoken needs or desires that go unfulfilled. Past, unresolved issues can resurface, adding layers of tension to current disagreements. These lingering problems can act like ticking time bombs, ready to ignite at any moment. Additionally, stress and external pressures, such as work-related worries or family obligations, can exacerbate these triggers, making conflicts more intense and frequent. Identifying these common triggers is the first step in addressing them, allowing you to approach conflicts with a clearer understanding of their origins.

Recognizing personal conflict triggers requires introspection and proactive strategies. Keeping a trigger journal can be an effective way to track and identify patterns. By noting down instances of conflict and reflecting on the emotions and situations involved, you can start to see recurring themes. Reflective exercises, such as meditation or guided visualization, can also help you gain insight into your emotional responses and identify potential triggers. Engaging in open discussions with your partner or a therapist about these triggers can provide valuable perspectives and support. These conversations can help you understand your triggers and your partner's, fostering a more empathetic and collaborative approach to conflict resolution.

Consider this couple, Lisa and Rick, who often clashed over finances. Each month, the budgeting stress led to overwhelming and upsetting arguments. By identifying financial stress as a key trigger, they could address it directly. They began scheduling regular financial check-ins, creating a space for open discussion and joint decision-making. This proactive approach transformed their financial discussions from battlegrounds into opportunities for collaboration. Another example involves a couple who frequently argued about household responsibilities. By recognizing that unmet expectations were at the core of their conflicts, they implemented a chore schedule, clearly outlining each person's duties. This clarity reduced misunderstandings and helped them manage their household more effectively.

Interactive Element: Conflict Trigger Checklist

Create a checklist in your notebook to help identify your personal conflict triggers. Include categories such as emotional, situational, and external stressors. Reflect on past conflicts and consider what might have triggered them. This checklist can be valuable in recognizing and addressing triggers before they escalate into full-blown arguments. Use this resource to foster greater self-awareness and improve your approach to conflict resolution.

5.2 Techniques for De-Escalating Arguments

When arguments start to heat up, emotion makes it easy to feel swept away. Words fly, voices rise, and a simple disagreement has become a full-blown conflict before you know it. De-escalation techniques become invaluable because they provide tools to guide the conversation back to a calmer state. Taking a timeout is one of the most effective strategies. Just as an athlete pauses to regroup during a game, stepping away from a heated argument lets you cool down and gain perspective. It's not about avoiding the issue but creating space to think clearly. Deep breathing exercises are another powerful tool. Focusing on your breath can calm your nervous system, reducing stress and anxiety in the moment. This simple act can help you maintain a calm and steady tone, signaling to your partner that you're willing to work through the disagreement thoughtfully rather than reactively.

Implementing these techniques requires awareness and practice. Recognizing the signs of escalation is the first step. Pay attention to physical cues—like increased heart rate or tension—and emotional signals, such as feeling overwhelmed or defensive. Once you notice these signs, it's time to act. Agreeing on a safe word or signal with your partner for timeouts can be incredibly helpful. This pre-arranged cue indicates that you can pause the conversation without fear of rejection or escalation. It's an agreement that prioritizes the relationship over the argument.

During these moments, practicing active listening becomes crucial. Even when tensions are high, focus on hearing your partner's concerns without planning your rebuttal. Exercising patience and restraint can work wonders, transforming conflict into collaboration. It's a powerful approach that reshapes the conversation for the better.

Managing emotions is crucial in preventing escalation. Emotional regulation is about controlling your feelings rather than letting them control you. Techniques for self-soothing, such as visualization or progressive muscle relaxation, can effectively calm your mind and body. The impact of emotional regulation on conflict outcomes is profound. When you manage your emotions, you're more likely to articulate your thoughts clearly and listen actively, leading to more constructive outcomes. It doesn't mean you suppress your feelings but rather express them in a way that invites understanding and resolution. By fostering emotional regulation, you create an environment where both partners feel safe to express themselves without fear of judgment or retaliation.

Consider a scenario where a couple, Alex and Jamie, are in the midst of a heated argument about weekend plans. Sensing the rising tension, Alex suggests taking a timeout. They both agree on a 15-minute break, during which Alex practices deep breathing while Jamie goes for a walk. When they reconvene, the atmosphere is noticeably calmer. They could discuss their plans, and each offered compromises to respect the other's needs. Taking a simple break to compose and calm yourself is a powerful, yet simple technique.

In another example, imagine a couple at the dinner table, and their discussion quickly becomes a disagreement. One partner, feeling their frustration mounting, consciously slows their breathing. This small act helps them maintain a steady tone, preventing the argument from escalating further. These real-life scenarios demonstrate the power of de-escalation techniques in transforming conflict into an opportunity for growth and connection. Integrating these strategies into your interactions allows you to navigate disagreements with grace and empathy, strengthening your relationships.

5.3 Finding Win-Win Solutions

Finding a win-win solution during conflicts can transform the dynamics from adversarial to cooperative in any relationship. A win-win solution is an outcome where both parties feel satisfied with the resolution, as it addresses the needs and interests of everyone involved. This approach shifts the focus from winning an argument to finding a mutually beneficial resolution that strengthens the relationship in the long run. The relationship grows more resilient when both partners feel heard and valued, fostering trust and cooperation. The benefits of such solutions extend beyond the immediate issue, reinforcing the foundation of the relationship and promoting a collaborative spirit.

To reach a win-win solution, start by identifying shared goals and interests. Understanding what both parties value and aim to achieve is essential. Once we clearly understand these commonalities, let's work together to brainstorm multiple solutions. Encourage creativity and open-mindedness—sometimes, the best solutions come from unexpected ideas. After listing potential solutions, evaluate the options together. Consider the pros and cons of each, keeping in mind the shared goals you've identified. This step ensures both partners have a say in decision-making, increasing the likelihood of mutual satisfaction. By working through this structured approach, you can transform conflicts into opportunities for growth and connection.

Effective negotiation and compromise are vital skills in reaching a win-win solution. Using collaborative language is crucial. Phrases like "What if we tried this..." or "How about we consider..." invite dialogue rather than dictating terms. This language fosters a sense of partnership and collaboration. Finding common ground is another important aspect. Focus on areas of agreement rather than dwelling on differences. Acknowledging shared values or goals can bridge gaps and create a foundation for compromise. Being flexible and open-minded is also essential. Sometimes, a solution might require adjusting expectations or priorities.

Approach the negotiation with a willingness to adapt and find a balance that respects both partners' needs.

Consider the story of Emma and Taylor, who frequently clashed over financial decisions. Emma valued saving for the future, while Taylor preferred enjoying the present. By identifying their shared goal of financial security, they brainstormed options that allowed them to save and enjoy occasional treats. They agreed on a budget that allocated a portion of their income for savings while setting aside funds for leisure activities. This compromise respected both their values and strengthened their relationship.

Similarly, Sarah and Jamie struggled with household responsibilities, often leading to resentment and frustration. By negotiating their roles and responsibilities, they found a win-win solution that balanced their workloads. They created a chore schedule that played to each other's strengths, ensuring fairness and reducing tension.

These examples illustrate the power of win-win solutions in resolving conflicts. By focusing on mutual satisfaction, relationships can thrive, becoming more harmonious and supportive. These strategies resolve the dispute and enhance understanding and respect between partners. As you incorporate these techniques into your interactions, you'll discover that conflicts become opportunities for growth and connection, enriching your relationships with each resolved disagreement.

5.4 Rebuilding Trust After Conflicts

In the aftermath of conflict, rebuilding trust is crucial. Without trust, a relationship can feel like a house built on shaky ground. Trust provides the emotional security that partners need to feel safe and valued. It is the foundation that supports long-term stability in any relationship. When trust has been broken, whether by a misunderstanding or a more significant breach like infidelity, it disrupts this foundation, leaving both partners feeling vulnerable and uncertain. Rebuilding trust involves more than just time; it requires effort, honesty, and a willingness to address the damage head-on. It's about restoring the lost faith and reaffirming the commitment to the relationship's future.

The process of rebuilding trust begins with acknowledging the breach. Accountability involves owning up to the actions that caused harm without downplaying or shifting responsibility. Acknowledgment is the first step in showing your partner that you understand the impact of your actions. Following this, offering a sincere apology is vital. An apology is more than words; it expresses genuine remorse and a commitment to making amends. It involves a promise to change behavior and prevent future transgressions. Consistent and reliable behavior reinforces this promise, demonstrating that you are committed to rebuilding trust through actions, not just words. This consistency is vital, as it helps slowly restore the damaged foundation of trust, showing your partner that they can rely on you again. Open and transparent communication further supports this process, creating a space for honesty and understanding. By communicating openly, both partners can express their feelings and concerns, fostering a sense of safety and connection.

Forgiveness plays a pivotal role in rebuilding trust. It involves letting go of past grievances and moving forward with a positive mindset. Forgiveness is not about forgetting or excusing the behavior that caused the breach; instead, it's about releasing the hold that anger and resentment have on you. This release allows for healing and growth, both individually and within the relationship. Forgiving opens the door to rebuilding a healthier, more resilient connection. It's a personal decision that requires patience and understanding, but it is essential for genuine reconciliation and the restoration of trust.

Consider this story of a couple navigating the aftermath of infidelity. The unfaithful partner took full responsibility for their actions, acknowledging the pain they caused. They offered a heartfelt apology and committed to transparency, allowing their partner to ask questions and express their feelings. Over time, with consistent and trustworthy behavior, they began to rebuild the fractured trust. Their story shows that hard work and commitment can fix even big mistakes. It's a powerful example of transformation.

Another example involves a couple who experienced a heated argument that left emotional scars. By openly discussing the incident and expressing forgiveness, they were able to move past the hurt and emerge with a stronger bond. The following examples show how relationships can exhibit resilience when intentionally and thoughtfully restoring trust.

In essence, rebuilding trust is about more than words. It's about intentional actions and emotional healing. You can restore the trust that holds your relationship together through acknowledgment, apology, consistent behavior, and open communication. Forgiveness is the glue that binds these efforts, allowing you to let go of past hurts and embrace a future of renewed connection. Remember that trust plays a crucial role in building a solid relationship. With commitment and understanding, you can rebuild it even stronger than before as you navigate through this process.

Please Consider Leaving a Review

Make a Difference with Your Review

By leaving an honest review of *The Path to Healthy Relationships* on Amazon, you can help others improve communication, build emotional connections, and resolve conflicts more effectively. Your feedback can guide someone else toward stronger, healthier relationships.

Your review could help:

- One more couple to communicate better.

- One more friend develops deeper connections.

- One more colleague resolves conflicts.

Scan the QR code for the USA or go to Amazon in the country where you purchased it and leave your review today!

Thank you, I appreciate your support!

Chapter 6

Establishing and Maintaining Boundaries

Picture yourself gathering with friends at a bustling café. The chatter swells around you as you sip your coffee, and you're caught up in the lively exchange of stories and laughter. Yet, as the conversation turns personal, you find yourself pulling back, feeling the need for solitude amidst the crowd. This instinct to retreat highlights the invisible lines we draw our limits. Just as physical barriers define our personal space, personal limits delineate the emotional, mental, and temporal boundaries that protect our well-being. Understanding these limits is crucial for maintaining healthy relationships and ensuring we remain balanced and content with our interactions.

Personal limits are the boundaries we set to define acceptable and unacceptable in our interactions. They encompass various aspects of our lives, including physical boundaries that determine personal space, emotional boundaries that safeguard against emotional labor, mental boundaries that protect our intellectual privacy, and time boundaries that manage how we allocate our time. Physical boundaries, for instance, involve maintaining personal space in crowded settings or choosing whom we feel comfortable hugging. Emotional boundaries help us manage the emotional energy we invest in relationships, ensuring we don't become overwhelmed by others' needs. Mental boundaries protect our thoughts and beliefs, allowing us to remain independent. Time boundaries ensure we prioritize our time effectively, balancing personal needs with external demands.

Recognizing and respecting personal limits is essential for preventing burnout and resentment. We risk overextending ourselves when we fail to acknowledge these boundaries, leading to mental and physical exhaustion. You might notice signs of boundary violations when you start feeling overwhelmed or resentful, indicators that you're stretching yourself too thin. Overextending yourself can manifest as saying "yes" too often, neglecting self-care, or feeling guilty for prioritizing your needs. This continual compromise erodes your sense of self and can lead to resentment towards others who demand more than you can give. By understanding the impact of overstepping your limits, you can take steps to protect your well-being and foster more balanced, fulfilling interactions.

To identify your limits, engage in self-reflection exercises encouraging introspection and awareness. Spend time contemplating what truly matters to you and where you feel most drained. Keeping a boundary journal can be invaluable, enabling you to track instances where boundaries were violated. Reflect on these occurrences to identify patterns and areas that need increased attention. Consulting with a therapist or counselor can also provide guidance and support, offering an external perspective that can help clarify your boundaries. These methods empower you to recognize your limits and make informed decisions about how to uphold them.

Consider the story of Maya, a dedicated professional who found herself constantly saying "yes" to extra projects at work. Over time, she realized she was sacrificing her personal life for work commitments, leading to resentment and exhaustion. By keeping a boundary journal, Maya identified her tendency to prioritize work over personal time. She began setting clear limits on her availability, ensuring she left work at a reasonable hour to pursue her hobbies. Similarly, imagine living in a bustling city where personal space is a luxury. Learning to set physical boundaries, like choosing when to engage socially or retreating to a quiet corner, can preserve your sense of autonomy and peace. Recognizing and acting on these limits fosters a healthier balance in life, allowing you to engage more fully and authentically with the world around you.

6.2 Communicating Boundaries Assertively

In every relationship, assertive communication is the guiding compass, steering you toward mutual understanding and harmony. It helps you express your needs clearly, reducing misunderstandings and promoting mutual respect. Imagine you're in a conversation where your needs seem to get lost in translation.

You feel frustrated but express your boundaries assertively instead of retreating into silence or lashing out. This approach allows you to stand firm without being aggressive, creating a space where both parties feel respected and understood. Assertive communication involves finding a balance in making your voice heard without overshadowing others. It's essential for maintaining healthy boundaries, as it ensures your needs are respected while respecting the boundaries of those around you.

To communicate assertively, start by using "I" statements. These statements focus on your feelings rather than blaming others, reducing defensiveness and inviting open dialogue. For example, saying, "I need some quiet time after work to recharge," communicates your need without casting blame. Being transparent and specific about your needs is also essential. Avoid vague language and be direct about what you require. This clarity helps others understand your boundaries and fosters cooperation. Remaining calm and composed is another crucial aspect. Maintaining a steady tone and demeanor promotes constructive conversation even when emotions run high. This calmness signals that you're open to collaboration rather than confrontation, encouraging a positive outcome.

To practice assertive communication, engage in role-playing scenarios where you set boundaries in various contexts. This exercise allows you to explore different situations and refine your approach. You might role-play a scenario where you must communicate time boundaries with a partner, practicing expressing your needs without causing conflict. Written exercises can also be beneficial. Take some time to draft boundary statements related to everyday situations you encounter. For example, write down how to address a friend who frequently interrupts your time. These exercises reinforce your skills and build confidence in asserting your boundaries effectively.

Real-life scenarios provide valuable insights into assertive communication. Consider the story of Sarah, who often felt overwhelmed by her social commitments. Recognizing the need for change, she began communicating her time boundaries with friends. By saying, "I value our time together, but I also need some evenings to myself," she could assert her needs without damaging her relationships. Her friends respected her honesty, making their interactions more balanced and fulfilling. In another case, imagine Jason, who struggled with emotional boundaries at work. By expressing his need for space during lunch breaks, he found a way to recharge and remain productive throughout the day. These examples illustrate how assertive communication can transform interactions, ensuring boundaries are respected while maintaining healthy and fulfilling relationships.

6.3 Respecting Others' Boundaries

Respecting others' boundaries is foundational to building relationships rooted in trust and understanding. When you honor the limits set by others, you create a safe space where both parties feel valued and respected. It's about recognizing that each individual has their comfort zones and needs that deserve acknowledgment. This mutual respect fosters a deeper connection in any relationship, allowing both individuals to engage authentically and without fear of judgment. When boundaries are respected, the relationship flourishes, growing stronger and more resilient. This respect isn't just a passive acknowledgment but an active practice that involves being attentive and considerate in your interactions.

Recognizing boundaries can be a nuanced skill, but it begins with paying close attention to nonverbal cues. These signals often reveal more than words, offering insights into how someone feels. A friend stepping back as the conversation gets more intense or a colleague crossing their arms during a meeting might indicate discomfort. Observing these cues requires attentiveness and sensitivity, allowing you to adjust your behavior accordingly. If you ever feel uncertain about whether you might be crossing a boundary, feel free to ask for clarification. Simple questions like, "Is this okay with you?" can make a significant difference. This approach shows that you prioritize their comfort and consent, reinforcing trust and understanding.

Guidelines for respecting boundaries are straightforward yet powerful. Always get permission, especially in personal or sensitive situations. Permission could be anything from borrowing something from someone to starting a serious conversation. Seeking consent ensures that the other person feels in control and respected. Avoid overstepping limits by being mindful of the cues and feedback you receive and the context of your relationship.

Additionally, cultural differences can influence boundaries, so remain sensitive to these variations. What might be acceptable in one culture could be intrusive in another. Being aware of these differences helps maintain respect and prevents misunderstandings.

Real-life examples highlight the positive impact of respecting boundaries. Take the story of Mark, who realized his partner needed alone time after a hectic day. He strengthened their bond by giving her space and understanding her need for solitude, fostering a sense of security and respect. Their relationship flourished as both partners felt heard and valued. Another example involves navigating cultural boundaries in a diverse workplace. Imagine a team that includes members from various cultural backgrounds. The team cultivated an inclusive environment where everyone felt respected and valued by actively listening to each member's preferences and being open to learning. These examples illuminate how respecting boundaries can transform interactions, leading to healthier and more fulfilling relationships.

6.4 Handling Boundary Violations

When someone disregards your boundaries, it can feel like a breach in the very fabric of your relationship. The erosion of trust is often the first casualty as you question whether your needs and feelings are valued. This breach can lead to increased conflict and resentment, creating a cycle of tension that is difficult to break. When boundaries have been crossed, it can feel like a personal attack, causing an emotional rift. Once trust is broken, it isn't easy to rebuild, and the relationship suffers. It is essential to address these breaches to prevent further harm and restore harmony. The first step in addressing a boundary violation is recognizing it. Understanding the profound impact on your emotional and mental state when someone breaches your comfort zone is essential. Identifying and assertively communicating the issue is crucial. Approach the conversation calmly, expressing what boundary was crossed and how it impacted you. Setting clear consequences if the violation continues is essential, establishing that your boundaries are non-negotiable. These consequences are not threats but necessary measures to protect your well-being. They serve as a reminder that your needs deserve respect and consideration.

Maintaining boundaries after addressing violations requires consistency and, sometimes, external support. Consistently reinforcing your boundaries lets others know you are serious about your limits. Remember to set gentle reminders and stand firm when your boundaries are tested. Support from friends, family, or professionals can give you extra strength and perspective. External support can validate and advise, helping you handle difficult situations confidently. It's a team effort to maintain your boundaries and ensure they are respected in all interactions.

Consider a case study of Sophie and her friend, Lily. Sophie often felt drained after their interactions because Lily would frequently overstep emotional boundaries, turning every conversation into a personal coun-seling session. Sophie, recognizing the violation, decided to address the issue assertively. She explained to Lily that while she valued their friend-ship, she needed their conversations to be more balanced. Sophie set a consequence: if Lily continued to monopolize the discussions, she would limit their interactions. By consistently reinforcing this boundary, Sophie found that their conversations became more reciprocal and enjoyable.

In another example, imagine dealing with a difficult family member who continually imposes their opinions on personal matters. You can maintain your autonomy by setting clear boundaries and repeating them as necessary. You might say, "I appreciate your concern, but I need to make my own decisions," and consistently uphold this stance. Over time, with patience and persistence, your boundaries become respected, even by those who once disregarded them.

Establishing and maintaining boundaries is a form of self-care and a vital component of healthy relationships. As you navigate boundary violations, remember that your needs and limits are valid and deserve respect. Handling these challenges with assertiveness and consistency leads to more authentic connections and deeper trust, paving the way for healthier interactions. With these tools, you can foster relationships that honor both your boundaries and the ones set by others, ensuring mutual respect and understanding.

Chapter 7

Emotional Reconnection Practices for Couples

Imagine coming home after a long day, your mind swirling with the day's events. You and your partner settle into your evening routine, but something feels off and you are distracted. The connection you once felt seems distant, overshadowed by the hustle of daily life. Many couples face this scenario, where the demands of work, family, and other commitments slowly erode the emotional bond vital to a thriving relationship. This chapter explores simple yet effective practices to rekindle that connection, starting with a powerful tool: daily check-ins.

Daily check-ins are brief, intentional conversations designed to foster a consistent emotional connection between partners. They are an opportunity to pause, step away from the chaos of life, and focus on one another. Setting aside a few moments each day creates a space where both partners can express their feelings, share their experiences, and address concerns. This practice helps prevent misunderstandings from escalating into conflicts as you address issues before they become entrenched. Moreover, daily check-ins provide a platform for both partners to express their thoughts and emotions, ensuring that neither feel overlooked or unheard. This consistent communication builds trust and understanding, strengthening the relationship over time.

Establishing a simple, repeatable structure to implement daily check-ins effectively is helpful. Begin by setting a specific time each day that works for both partners, whether over breakfast, during a walk, or before bed. Consistency is key, reinforcing the habit and ensuring that both partners prioritize this time together. Start each check-in with positive reflections, sharing moments of gratitude or joy from the day, setting a positive tone, and fostering appreciation for one another. Then, move on to discussing any concerns or issues that may have arisen. Encourage open, honest dialogue, focusing on understanding rather than blame. Conclude with expressions of appreciation or affirmations, reinforcing the emotional connection and leaving both partners feeling valued and supported.

As you engage in daily check-ins, consider incorporating specific questions to guide the conversation. Asking about the best part of your partner's day invites them to share positive experiences, fostering a sense of gratitude and connection. Inquiring if anything has been on their mind lately opens the door for honest dialogue and emotional support. Asking how you can better support them demonstrates a willingness to meet their needs and strengthen the partnership. These questions facilitate meaningful conversations and help both partners feel understood and appreciated, enhancing the relationship dynamic.

Real-life examples highlight the transformative power of daily check-ins. Take Sarah and John, a couple who found themselves drifting apart amid the demands of work and family. By committing to a nightly check-in, they addressed minor issues before they escalated and rediscovered the emotional connection they once cherished. Sarah recalls how setting aside time to talk made her feel more understood and supported, transforming their relationship. Another couple, Emily and James, integrated daily check-ins into their morning routine, sharing a cup of coffee while discussing their plans for the day. This practice strengthened their bond and set a positive tone for the day ahead.

Interactive Element: Daily Check-In Checklist

Create a checklist in your notebook to guide your daily check-ins. Include prompts for positive reflections, concerns, and affirmations. Use this tool to ensure your conversations remain focused and meaningful, enhancing your emotional connection and fostering a supportive relationship environment. Consistently engaging in this practice can transform your relationship, creating a foundation of trust, understanding, and emotional intimacy.

7.2 Shared Activities to Foster Closeness

Life can sometimes feel like a series of routines and responsibilities, often leaving little room for the spontaneity and joy that once defined your relationship. Sharing activities is a beautiful way to rekindle the bond and create lasting memories. When you and your partner participate in activities together, it promotes teamwork and cooperation. Whether tackling a new recipe in the kitchen or navigating a hiking trail, these moments require collaboration and communication. They teach you to rely on each other, strengthening the partnership as you work toward a common goal. But it's not all hard work; shared activities also bring opportunities for joy and fun. Laughter and shared triumphs over a challenging task can reignite the spark that first brought you together, reminding you of the pleasure in each other's company. As you collect these experiences, they weave into the tapestry of your shared history, enriching your relationship with a reservoir of fond memories.

Consider introducing a variety of activities into your routine to foster closeness. Cooking or baking together is a simple yet effective way to spend quality time. Whether creating a gourmet meal or simply baking cookies, the process encourages cooperation and creativity. Walking or hiking offers a chance to connect with nature and each other, providing a peaceful setting for conversation and reflection. Engaging in a shared hobby, like painting or gardening, can be particularly rewarding. These activities allow you to explore mutual interests and discover new passions together. The key is to choose activities that you both enjoy and that facilitate interaction and engagement. These shared experiences lay the groundwork for a deeper connection as you learn more about each other's strengths, preferences, and quirks.

Stepping out of your comfort zone to try new activities together can further enhance your relationship. Introducing novelty and excitement keeps the dynamic fresh and invigorating, preventing stagnation in long-term partnerships. Trying something new, such as signing up for a dance class or attempting a new sport, encourages mutual support and learning. You'll find yourselves cheering each other on, celebrating successes, and laughing at the inevitable missteps. These experiences foster a spirit of adventure and curiosity, reminding you of the joy of discovery. Embracing new challenges together can also reveal hidden talents and interests, opening doors to further exploration and growth as a couple.

Real-life stories highlight the impact of shared activities on relationship strength. Take Sam and Alex, who decided to learn a new language together. As they practiced vocabulary and phrases, they laughed at their mispronunciations and celebrated each other's progress. This shared goal brought them closer and gave them a new way to communicate and connect. Another couple, Lisa and Mark, committed to weekly date nights, each taking turns planning a surprise activity. Whether attending a pottery class or exploring a new restaurant, these evenings became cherished rituals that reignited their connection. Lisa recalls how these shared adventures reminded her of the excitement of their early days together, deepening their bond and reinforcing their commitment.

7.3 Intimate Conversations Beyond the Surface

Imagine sitting across from your partner, sharing a meal, or simply relaxing together. The conversation flows effortlessly at first, filled with the usual talk of work, errands, and weekend plans. But beneath these surface-level exchanges lies an opportunity for a deeper connection—a chance to know each other at the core. Intimate conversations go beyond the mundane, building emotional intimacy and trust. They invite vulnerability and openness, creating a safe space where you can explore each other's deeper thoughts and feelings. These discussions can transform your relationship into a sanctuary of understanding and empathy.

Initiating such meaningful conversations requires intention and care. Start by asking open-ended questions, encouraging your partner to share more than facts or opinions. Questions like "What are your biggest dreams and aspirations?" or "What is a childhood memory that shaped who you are today?" can open doors to profound insights. As you ask, create an environment that feels safe and non-judgmental. Let your partner know that their thoughts and feelings are welcome, free from criticism or dismissal. Being fully present is crucial—put aside distractions, make eye contact, and listen with genuine interest. Your attentiveness signals that you value what they say, fostering a sense of closeness and trust.

To help guide these conversations, consider prompts that invite reflection and depth. Ask, "What are some of your fears or is there anything you might be worried about?" or "What do you envision for our future together?" These questions reveal personal landscapes and strengthen your understanding of one another. As you explore these topics, remain open and receptive, allowing the conversation to flow naturally. Share your thoughts and feelings in response, creating a reciprocal exchange and deepening your bond. The goal is to emerge from these dialogues with a richer appreciation of each other's inner worlds.

Real-life scenarios illustrate the profound impact of intimate conversations. Take Laura and Mike, who decided to dedicate one evening a week to such discussions. They began by reminiscing about their childhoods and sharing stories and experiences that shaped who they are today. As they talked, they discovered new facets of each other—dreams and fears that had never surfaced. This practice brought them closer, enriching their relationship with newfound empathy and understanding. Another couple, Rachel and Sam, found solace in nightly talks, where they shared everything from life goals to unspoken insecurities. These conversations became a cherished ritual, a time to connect and support one another in ways they hadn't before.

The benefits of these deep connections are manifold. Couples who embrace intimate conversations report feeling more understood and appreciated. They experience a heightened sense of trust, knowing their partner truly sees and values them. This depth of connection can also enhance conflict resolution, as partners are more attuned to each other's perspectives and emotions. When you know and understand your partner on this level, you can approach challenges with empathy and compassion, fostering a more harmonious partnership. The richness of these conversations transcends every day, weaving a tapestry of love and understanding that fortifies your relationship against the storms of life.

7.4 Bids for Connection

In the dance of daily life, amidst routines and responsibilities, partners often make unconscious efforts to connect emotionally. These are known as "bids for connection." These small gestures are crucial for maintaining and deepening emotional bonds. Picture a partner offering a simple smile across the room, a touch on the shoulder while passing by, or a casual request for advice on a trivial matter. Each action is a bid to seek affection, affirmation, or attention from the other. They serve as the building blocks of emotional intimacy, quietly nurturing the relationship by fostering a sense of closeness and understanding. Such bids may seem mundane, yet they hold the power to strengthen the emotional fabric that ties partners together.

Recognizing and responding to these bids is vital for a healthy relationship. But how do you spot them? It starts with paying attention to both verbal and non-verbal cues. A partner might say, "Look at this funny video," or sigh after a long day at work. Each is a bid for your presence and engagement. Responding with genuine interest is critical. Turning toward your partner when they reach out, rather than away, signals that you value their attempt to connect. Whether sharing a laugh at that video or offering a comforting word after that sigh, these moments of acknowledgment convey that you are present and attentive. They affirm your commitment to fostering a supportive and loving environment, allowing emotional intimacy to flourish.

Conversely, consistently ignoring or dismissing these bids can have negative consequences. Over time, it can lead to an erosion of emotional intimacy, leaving one or both partners feeling neglected or unloved. Imagine a partner consistently dismissing attempts at conversation or affection; the result is often a growing sense of rejection and loneliness, leading to resentment, slowly eroding the foundation of the relationship. It's a gradual process that can transform a once vibrant connection into a shadow of its former self. Recognizing and valuing bids cannot be overstated, as they are fundamental to sustaining a thriving relationship.

Consider the story of Jenna and Tom, who found their relationship strained due to busy schedules. They realized they needed to include each other's bids for connection. Tom habitually shared his thoughts about the day, while Jenna often sought his opinion on her creative projects. By acknowledging these bids, they managed to rekindle their emotional connection. On the other hand, Lisa and Mark struggled when Mark's frequent bids for attention went unnoticed. He often tried to engage Lisa in conversations about mutual interests, but her distracted responses led to feelings of isolation. Recognizing the issue, they started setting aside dedicated time for each other, improving their communication and bringing them closer.

Bids for connection may seem small, but they are significant in nurturing emotional bonds. Recognizing and responding to these bids can transform and enrich your relationship. As we conclude this chapter, remember that these small gestures build the foundation of love and understanding. The next chapter will explore how balancing independence and togetherness can strengthen your relationship, offering practical strategies for maintaining personal space and shared intimacy.

Chapter 8

Balancing Independence and Togetherness

Picture this scenario: a couple sits together at the breakfast table, calendars spread out, each organizing their day or week. The hustle of life pulls them in different directions—work demands, social obligations, personal interests—yet here they are, seeking harmony amidst the chaos. This scene is familiar, a testament to the delicate dance of balancing independence with togetherness in relationships. It's a balance that requires attention and intention, where time becomes both an ally and a challenge. Successfully managing this balance hinges on a crucial skill: time management. Without it, the hustle can quickly lead to stress, and the togetherness you desire can fade into a distant memory.

Effective time management is crucial for harmonizing personal needs with relationship goals. It's not just about squeezing more activities into your day; it's about making deliberate choices that prevent burnout and foster well-being. When managed well, time becomes a tool for ensuring that you nurture both personal growth and relational bonds. It allows you to reserve personal reflection and relaxation moments without compromising the time needed to connect with your partner. This balance helps maintain mental clarity and prevent the overwhelming feelings that can arise when everything seems to demand your attention at once.

To manage time efficiently, consider adopting practical strategies that empower you to take control of your schedule. One helpful approach is using calendars or planners to organize personal and shared activities. Having a calendar on the fridge is a great idea. You can prioritize personal and relationship needs by scheduling 'me time' and 'us time' on a weekly calendar. This visual representation of your time helps prevent overcommitment and allows you to see at a glance where adjustments might be needed. Prioritizing activities based on importance and urgency is another crucial technique. Recognize which tasks require immediate attention and which can be scheduled for later, allowing you to focus on what matters most.

Communication is pivotal in effective time management, especially when balancing personal and relationship needs. Regularly updating each other on schedules and commitments fosters transparency and reduces the risk of misunderstandings. Consider setting aside time for monthly meetings where both partners can discuss upcoming activities and make necessary adjustments. This practice ensures that both parties are well-informed and promotes flexibility and accommodation, making it easy to manage unexpected changes. Proactively discussing time management strategies helps align priorities and maintain harmony within the relationship.

Incorporating practical tools can further enhance your time management efforts. Time-blocking techniques, where you allocate specific blocks of time for different activities, can help you maintain focus and productivity. Time management apps like Google Calendar or Todoist can streamline your scheduling process, allowing you to set reminders and share calendars with your partner. This shared approach to planning ensures that both partners are aware of each other's commitments and can plan joint activities accordingly. Creating a shared online calendar for activities like date nights or family events ensures that these important moments are included in our busy daily lives.

Interactive Element: Time Management Reflection Exercise

Spend a few minutes reflecting on your current time management practices. Consider areas where you feel overwhelmed or where your personal and relationship needs might be out of balance. Write down three specific actions to improve your time management, focusing on individual and shared activities. This exercise will help you identify opportunities for growth and alignment, fostering a more harmonious balance between independence and togetherness.

8.2 Personal Space Agreements

In any relationship, maintaining individuality while nurturing togetherness is a delicate balance. Personal space agreements are an effective way to achieve this balance. These agreements are mutual understandings that respect each person's need for solitude and independence. They prevent feelings of suffocation or neglect by ensuring that both partners have the freedom to recharge and pursue personal interests. Think of it as a safety net that protects your individuality without compromising your connection. It's about recognizing that time alone doesn't mean disconnection but rather an opportunity to return to the relationship refreshed and re-energized.

Creating personal space agreements involves a thoughtful approach. Start by having an open discussion about individual needs and preferences. Each partner should express what kind of personal space they require and why it matters. This conversation is crucial as it lays the groundwork for understanding and empathy. Once needs are articulated, set clear and respectful boundaries; for example, you might agree on specific hours during the day where time alone is respected, allowing each person to engage in personal activities without interruption. These boundaries should be flexible enough to adapt to changing circumstances but firm enough to provide a sense of security.

Respecting personal space agreements is an ongoing practice. Avoid interrupting your partner during their designated alone time. This respect shows that you value their need for independence. Periodically check in with each other to ensure that the agreements still meet your needs and make adjustments as necessary. If one partner feels the current arrangement isn't working, discuss it openly and find a compromise. This ongoing dialogue reinforces the relationship's foundation of trust and mutual respect. Recognizing when adjustments are needed prevents resentment from building and keeps the relationship healthy and balanced.

Consider the story of Jennifer and Nathan , who both work from home. Initially, the constant proximity led to tension as they struggled to find personal space. They decided to establish personal space agreements by designating certain areas of their home as individual workspace zones. They also agreed on specific times for uninterrupted work. This structure allowed them to focus on their tasks while respecting each other's need for solitude. Another example involves Michelle and Mark, who realized the importance of personal space during stressful periods. They each set aside a few hours weekly to engage in solo activities they enjoyed, whether reading, jogging, or simply meditating. This practice helped them manage stress and strengthened their bond by returning to the relationship with renewed energy and appreciation for each other.

Personal space agreements are not about creating distance but about fostering independence within the context of a relationship. They allow each partner to maintain a sense of self while being part of a supportive unit. Acknowledging and respecting each other's space creates an environment where both partners can thrive individually and collectively. This balance of independence and togetherness enriches the relationship, making it more resilient and fulfilling.

8.3 Supporting Each Other's Interests

In any relationship, supporting each other's interests is a cornerstone for personal growth and fulfillment. When you encourage your partner in their hobbies or passions, you open the door to deeper understanding and connection. It's not just about allowing them the time and space to pursue what they love; it's about engaging with those interests, even if they are not yours. Doing so, you help cultivate an environment where both partners feel valued and respected. This encouragement fosters personal development, as each individual has the freedom to explore and expand their horizons. In turn, this growth positively impacts the relationship, enriching the experiences and perspectives both partners bring to the table. The relationship becomes a dynamic space where partners feel supported in their journey, leading to a stronger, more resilient bond.

Showing support for a partner's interests can take many forms, ranging from grand gestures to everyday actions. Attending events or activities related to their passions is one way to demonstrate this support. Whether it's a photography exhibit or a community theater performance, your presence sends a powerful message of encouragement. Even if the interest is not one you share, your willingness to engage shows that you value their happiness and fulfillment. Asking questions and genuine curiosity about their hobbies can also go a long way. It's about listening to what excites them and understanding the 'why' behind their pursuits. For instance, if your partner has taken up pottery, join them for a class or visit a local pottery show. The shared experience supports their interest, creates lasting memories, and strengthens your connection.

The benefits of mutual support in a relationship are profound. When both partners feel backed by the other, it increases emotional connection and fosters a sense of security. It's affirming to know that someone has your back, cheering you on as you pursue your dreams. This support also nurtures greater appreciation and respect for one another. As you grow through your interests, you gain insights into your partner's personality, values, and aspirations. This deeper understanding enriches the relationship, creating a foundation of mutual respect and admiration. Such a dynamic encourages both partners to be authentic, fostering a nurturing environment where love and respect thrive. The relationship becomes a partnership in the truest sense, where both individuals actively contribute to each other's happiness and success.

Real-life testimonials highlight the impact of supporting each other's interests. Take the story of Anna and David, who found themselves at a crossroads when David decided to switch careers and pursue his passion for culinary arts. Initially, Anna worried about the implications, but she supported him wholeheartedly. Her encouragement and belief in his abilities fueled his confidence, leading to his successful career change. Another example is Lisa and Tom, whose mutual encouragement led to significant personal achievements. Lisa initially hesitated when Tom expressed interest in hiking, but she joined him on his expeditions, discovering a newfound love for the outdoors. Their shared experiences strengthened their bond as they supported each other in new endeavors. These stories underscore the transformative power of mutual support, illustrating how a simple encouragement can lead to remarkable growth and deepen the connection between partners.

8.4 Maintaining Personal Hobbies and Passions

In the framework of life, personal hobbies and passions are the vibrant threads that weave a sense of identity and fulfillment. They offer a sanctuary from the demands of everyday life, a space where you can express creativity and find joy. Pursuing hobbies nurtures the soul and brings a sense of accomplishment and purpose. Engaging in activities you love can significantly reduce stress, providing relaxation and mental clarity. Whether painting, gardening, or playing an instrument, these pursuits offer a much-needed escape, allowing you to recharge and return to your relationships with renewed energy and positivity.

Balancing hobbies with relationship time, however, requires thoughtful consideration. It's essential to carve out dedicated time for your passions while ensuring your relationship thrives. Set aside specific times for your hobbies, perhaps during your partner's busy periods, to avoid feelings of neglect. Engaging in hobbies together occasionally can also be rewarding. It provides an opportunity to share experiences and create lasting memories. For instance, if you enjoy hiking, invite your partner to join you on a weekend trek. Doing so allows you to indulge in your interests and strengthens your bond through shared adventures.

Introducing new hobbies into your life should be approached with open communication. Express your desire to explore new activities, sharing your excitement and intentions with your partner. This transparency fosters understanding and prevents potential friction. Consider finding hobbies that you enjoy, both individually and together. For example, if you're interested in learning photography, you might take a class alone but plan weekend outings with your partner to practice your skills. This balance respects your individuality while nurturing your relationship.

Real-life stories often illustrate the successful integration of hobbies into relationships. Take the example of Laura, who rekindled her love for painting after years of not picking up a brush. Her partner, James, encouraged her by creating a small studio space in their home, offering support and understanding. Laura found fulfillment in her artistic expression, and the couple discovered a new level of closeness as James occasionally joined her in painting.

Another story involves Joe, a devoted cyclist struggling to balance his passion and relationship. Joe maintained his hobby and strengthened their connection by communicating his needs and inviting his partner on leisurely rides. These stories highlight the positive impact of balancing personal passions with relationship dynamics, showing that thriving with your interests and hobbies is possible while nurturing a shared life.

Incorporating personal hobbies into your life is not merely a luxury but a vital component of well-being. They enrich your sense of self and provide a buffer against the stresses of daily life. When balanced with relationship needs, hobbies enhance your connection with your partner, bringing vitality and joy to your shared journey. As we explore these themes, remember that maintaining your passions is an investment in your personal growth and your relationship's health. In the following chapter, we'll continue exploring the facets of a fulfilling relationship, focusing on navigating the complexities of emotional intelligence and self-awareness.

focusing on navigating the complexities of emotional intelligence and self-awareness.

Chapter 9

Understanding Toxic Patterns

Imagine a relationship where every interaction feels like walking on eggshells. You constantly second-guess your actions, wondering if a simple comment might provoke an unexpected reaction. This unsettling atmosphere is often a hallmark of toxic behaviors, which can subtly infiltrate relationships, leaving individuals feeling trapped and powerless. Toxic behaviors are those actions that undermine the foundation of healthy relationships, manifesting in various forms that can be both overt and insidious. At their core, these behaviors are detrimental to emotional and mental well-being, creating an environment of instability and distress.

Manipulation tactics are a common aspect of toxic behavior. Gaslighting, for instance, involves making someone doubt their perceptions, leaving them questioning their reality. It's a method of control that erodes trust and self-confidence. Guilt-tripping is another manipulative tactic, where one partner makes the other feel responsible for their emotions or actions, cultivating a sense of obligation and control. These tactics can leave you feeling emotionally drained and confused as if you're constantly navigating a minefield of expectations and disappointments.

Controlling behaviors often accompany manipulation, manifesting as isolation or micromanagement. Isolation may involve restricting your interactions with friends and family, creating a dependency on the toxic partner. On the other hand, micromanagement seeks to control every aspect of your life, from daily routines to personal decisions. These behaviors strip away your autonomy, fostering a sense of entrapment and helplessness. They are subtle yet pervasive, often justified as acts of care or concern but ultimately serving to tighten the reins of control.

Emotional abuse is another facet of toxic behavior characterized by criticism and belittling—negative comments, eroding self-esteem, and instilling self-doubt. Belittling may appear as jokes or sarcasm, masking genuine disdain or frustration. Over time, these actions chip away at your self-worth, leaving you feeling inadequate and devalued. The damage inflicted by emotional abuse can be profound, affecting how you perceive yourself and your place in the world.

Passive-aggressive actions, such as the silent treatment or back-handed compliments, are insidious yet damaging. The silent treatment freezes communication, leaving one partner in the dark, while back-handed compliments undermine confidence by couching criticism into false praise. These actions create an environment of uncertainty and tension, where genuine communication is stifled, and emotional distance grows. They are often used as tools to exert control without confrontation, leaving you feeling confused and isolated.

Imagine a partner who constantly checks your phone, questioning your every text and call. This behavior not only invades your privacy but also signals a lack of trust, fostering an atmosphere of suspicion and anxiety. Or consider a scenario where an individual publicly undermines your achievements, subtly diminishing your accomplishments in front of others. Such actions erode your confidence, making you second-guess your capabilities. Sarcasm, too, can mask genuine anger or frustration, creating a communication barrier where honesty is obscured by biting remarks.

The psychological impact of toxic behaviors is significant. They can lead to increased anxiety and stress levels, as you're perpetually on edge, anticipating the next conflict or manipulation. Your self-esteem and self-worth may suffer, as constant criticism and control make you doubt your value. Over time, this can result in feelings of isolation and loneliness, as the relationship's toxicity creates a barrier between you and others. You may withdraw and be disconnected from friends and loved ones who once provided support and solace.

Self-assessment is essential to recognize toxic behaviors in your relationships. Ask yourself if you often feel anxious, undervalued, or isolated. Consider whether you're frequently second-guessing your actions or avoiding specific topics to prevent conflict. A checklist of red flags, like those mentioned earlier, can help identify patterns of manipulation, control, or emotional abuse. Reflect on your emotional responses: do interactions leave you feeling drained or uplifted? Journaling can also be a powerful tool, tracking these patterns over time and offering insights into areas that need attention. Through these practices, you can gain clarity and address the toxic dynamics that may impact your well-being.

Self-Reflection Exercise

Take a moment to reflect on your relationships. Write down any instances where you felt manipulated, controlled, or belittled. Consider how these experiences made you feel and whether they are recurring patterns. Use this exercise as a starting point to identify areas where boundaries need to be set or strengthened.

9.2 Understanding the Impact of Toxic Patterns

Toxic patterns in relationships often unfold cyclically, creating a repetitive loop that can be challenging to break. It usually begins with the honeymoon phase, marked by a sense of reconciliation and temporary peace. During this time, the toxic partner may shower you with affection, apologies, and promises of change, giving you hope that the relationship will improve. This phase can be intoxicating, as it temporarily masks the underlying issues and rekindles the connection. However, the honeymoon phase often gives way to building tension. Subtle signs of discontent may begin to surface. Minor annoyances grow into more considerable grievances, and the underlying issues that were never truly resolved start to resurface. The tension builds gradually, creating an atmosphere of unease and anticipation. Eventually, this tension escalates to the point of explosion or crisis. Emotions boil over, leading to intense arguments or conflicts. The crisis point can be devastating, leaving you emotionally and mentally exhausted. Despite the turmoil, the cycle often concludes with a phase of reconciliation and false peace. Here, apologies may be exchanged, and temporary agreements may be made. However, without addressing the root causes of the toxicity, this peace is short-lived. The cycle resets, and the pattern begins anew, trapping individuals in a loop of hope, disappointment, and hurt.

The long-term effects of these toxic patterns on relationships can be profound and damaging. Trust and intimacy, the cornerstones of any healthy relationship, gradually erode under repeated conflicts and betrayals. You may question your partner's intentions, doubt their promises, and feel emotionally distant. The frequency and intensity of conflicts tend to increase over time as unresolved issues pile up. This escalating tension can lead to emotional burnout, where you become detached and numb to the relationship's dynamics. Emotional burnout is a state of exhaustion, where the constant cycle of emotional highs and lows leaves you feeling depleted and indifferent. The relationship, once vibrant and fulfilling, becomes a source of stress and anxiety.

Enduring toxic patterns not only affects relationships but also takes a significant toll on individual mental health. Continuous exposure to toxic dynamics can lead to depression and chronic anxiety. You might be overwhelmed by sadness, hopelessness, and constant worry. The emotional turmoil and stress can also contribute to the development of post-traumatic stress disorder (PTSD) or other trauma-related disorders. The persistent fear and hyper-vigilance in a toxic relationship can mirror the symptoms of PTSD, leaving lasting scars on your mental well-being. In an attempt to cope with the emotional pain, some individuals may turn to substance abuse, seeking temporary relief from the distress.

Unfortunately, this coping mechanism often exacerbates the situation, leading to further complications and dependencies.

Research and statistics underscore the seriousness of toxic patterns and their impact on mental health. Studies have shown that emotional abuse, a common component of toxic relationships, is prevalent and damaging. According to research, about 48% of women and 48% of men have experienced psychological aggression by an intimate partner in their lifetime. The psychological effects of toxic relationships can be long-lasting, affecting self-esteem, trust in others, and overall mental health. A study published in Psychology Today highlights that individuals who have experienced emotional abuse are at a higher risk of developing mental health issues such as depression, anxiety, and PTSD. These statistics emphasize the need to recognize and address toxic patterns, not only for the sake of the relationship but also for individual well-being. Professional help is often essential and most effective for addressing these types of abuse or mental health issues, ensuring the appropriate level of support is provided.

9.3 Breaking Free from Negative Cycles

Breaking free from toxic cycles requires a commitment to self-awareness and honesty. It starts with a candid evaluation of your relationship. Ask yourself if you feel valued and respected or if fear and anxiety dominate your interactions. Recognizing these patterns isn't about assigning blame but acknowledging reality. Observe your triggers and the responses they elicit. Are there recurring themes or situations that consistently lead to conflict? Understanding these dynamics is the first step toward change. This process demands courage, as it involves confronting uncomfortable truths about your relationship and your role in it. Yet, this clarity is empowering, paving the way for meaningful transformation.

Once you've identified these patterns, it's time to disrupt them. One effective strategy is setting immediate short-term goals for change. These goals could be as simple as committing to express your feelings openly or taking a step back when tensions rise. Implementing time-outs during conflicts is another practical approach. When emotions flare, stepping away lets both parties cool off and reflect before resuming the conversation. This break can prevent escalation and encourage more rational dialogue. Seeking external support and validation is equally important. Friends, family, or support groups can offer perspective, reminding you that you're not alone in this struggle. Their encouragement can bolster your resolve, providing the strength to challenge toxic patterns.

Professional help is invaluable in breaking these cycles. Therapy offers a safe space to explore your emotions and gain insights into your behavior. Individual therapy focuses on self-improvement, helping you develop healthier coping mechanisms and strengthen your emotional resilience. Couples counseling addresses relationship issues directly, facilitating communication and fostering understanding between partners. It provides tools to navigate conflicts constructively, encouraging collaboration rather than confrontation. Support groups, meanwhile, offer shared experiences and empathy, reinforcing that others have faced similar challenges and emerged stronger. These resources collectively support your journey toward healing, offering guidance and expertise when you need it most.

Consider the story of Anna and Tom, a couple trapped in a cycle of mistrust and resentment. They turned to therapy, where they learned to communicate openly and honestly. Through counseling, they identified the root causes of their conflicts and developed strategies to address them. Over time, they rebuilt trust and rediscovered their connection, transforming their relationship into one based on mutual respect and support. Then there's Rachel, who endured emotional abuse for years. With the guidance of a therapist, she recognized her worth and found the courage to leave the toxic relationship. Rachel's journey wasn't easy, but through therapy and the support of friends, she healed and regained her confidence. These stories demonstrate that breaking free from toxic cycles is possible. It requires effort and determination, but the rewards—freedom, peace, and healthier relationships—are worth every step.

9.4 The Role of Self-Awareness in Overcoming Toxicity

Self-awareness is akin to a mirror that reflects your true self, enabling you to see beyond the surface and recognize the underlying emotions and patterns that shape your behavior. It is the capacity to understand your feelings, triggers, and responses that play a crucial role in overcoming toxic behaviors. By gaining insight into what sets off your emotional reactions, you can identify how you might be contributing to unproductive dynamics. Anger flares up when you feel criticized, or withdrawal becomes a refuge when confronted with conflict. Recognizing these patterns is the first step in breaking the cycle of toxicity. This awareness allows you to take responsibility for your actions and make conscious choices that promote healthier interactions.

Self-reflection exercises are invaluable tools for cultivating self-awareness. Daily journaling prompts can guide you in exploring your thoughts and emotions, offering a structured way to track patterns over time. Consider questions like, "What emotions did I experience today, and why?" or "How did I react to stress, and what could I do differently?" These reflections can illuminate areas for growth and change. Meditation and mindfulness practices deepen self-awareness by encouraging you to be present with your feelings without judgment. Even a few minutes of focused breathing can help center your mind and bring clarity to your emotional landscape. Self-assessment quizzes are another resource, providing insights into your behavioral tendencies and how they might influence your relationships. These exercises, collectively, enhance your understanding of yourself and your interactions with others.

The impact of self-awareness on relationships is profound. As you become more attuned to your emotions, you improve your ability to regulate them. This emotional regulation reduces impulsive reactions, enabling you to respond thoughtfully rather than reactively. It fosters a sense of calm and control, which can diffuse potential conflicts before they escalate. Furthermore, self-awareness enhances empathy and understanding. By recognizing your vulnerabilities and needs, you become more sensitive to those of others, leading to deeper connections and more compassionate interactions. With better communication comes fewer misunderstandings as you learn to express your needs clearly and listen actively to others. These improvements enhance your current relationships and establish a basis for healthier ones in the future. Continuous self-improvement is a lifelong pursuit and can be easily approached with practical steps. Begin by incorporating self-reflection into your daily routine. Set aside time daily to reflect on your experiences and emotions through journaling, meditation, or quiet contemplation. This practice cultivates a habit of introspection, allowing you to assess your progress and recalibrate your goals regularly. Engage in ongoing learning by seeking feedback from trusted friends or professionals who can offer valuable perspectives on your behavior. Their insights can reveal blind spots and inspire growth. Finally, embrace a mindset of curiosity and openness. View challenges as opportunities to learn more about yourself and your relationships rather than obstacles to avoid. This approach nurtures resilience and adaptability, empowering you to navigate life's complexities with grace and insight.

Recognizing and enhancing self-awareness unlocks the potential for transformative change. It paves the way for breaking free from toxicity and fostering relationships grounded in mutual respect, empathy, and understanding. As you develop this awareness, you improve your interactions with others and deepen your relationship with yourself. This chapter has laid the groundwork for understanding how self-awareness can be a catalyst for change, setting the stage for exploring new ways to build meaningful, enriching connections.

Chapter 10

Healing from Past Traumas

Imagine walking through life carrying an invisible backpack, one that grows heavier with each unresolved issue and any unhealed wounds. Emotional baggage can feel like an unseen weight that affects how you interact with the world around you.

Emotional baggage refers to the unresolved issues from the past that cause emotional stress or pain. It encompasses the remnants of previous relationships, negative behavior patterns, and emotional triggers stemming from unprocessed experiences. These remnants persist, subtly and often unconsciously influencing your relationships. They show up as self-doubt, anxiety, or even anger, dictating your responses and interactions. While emotional baggage is akin to unprocessed trauma, it carries a unique connotation, often tied to feelings of guilt, regret, or fear.

Recognizing the signs that you might be carrying emotional baggage is the first step toward healing. Are you caught in recurring conflicts in new relationships, unable to break free from old patterns? Perhaps you overreact to minor issues, finding yourself disproportionately upset by small events. There might be your emotional baggage manifesting as heightened sensitivity. Trust may also be challenging to extend to partners, as past betrayals or disappointments cast a long shadow over present connections. These signs indicate that unhealed wounds influence your behavior, dictate your interactions, and create barriers to intimacy and trust. Acknowledging these patterns is not about self-blame but understanding how past experiences shape your present reality.

The impact of emotional baggage on relationships can be profound. Communication becomes strained as unresolved issues cloud your ability to express yourself clearly. Trust, the cornerstone of any healthy relationship, erodes when past betrayals linger unaddressed. This erosion fosters a fertile ground for conflicts, with misunderstandings and assumptions fueling disagreements. Over time, emotional baggage can create a cycle of tension and discord, making it difficult for relationships to thrive. The emotional weight you carry affects not only how you perceive others but also how you perceive yourself, leading to a cycle of negativity and disconnection. Recognizing and addressing this baggage is crucial for breaking free from these patterns and fostering healthier, more fulfilling connections.

Taking steps to address emotional baggage requires courage and commitment. Begin by acknowledging your past experiences and their impact on your current life. This acknowledgment is a powerful act of self-awareness, allowing you to identify the patterns and triggers that influence your behavior. Opening up to a trusted friend or partner can provide support and validation, creating a safe space for exploration. Seeking professional help is also valuable, as it offers guidance and tools for processing unresolved trauma. A therapist can help you unpack the layers of your experiences, providing a structured approach to healing. Through therapy, you can explore the roots of your emotional baggage, gaining insights and developing strategies for moving forward. This process is not about erasing the past but understanding and integrating it, enabling you to live more freely and authentically.

Reflection Section: Exploring Your Emotional Baggage

Take a moment to reflect on the patterns in your relationships. Are there recurring themes or triggers that persist? Consider writing down these observations, noting how they might connect to past experiences. This exercise can help you gain clarity and insight into your emotional baggage, serving as the first step in your journey towards healing and growth. Recognizing and addressing emotional baggage opens the door to healthier connections, allowing you to engage with others from a place of understanding and compassion.

10.2 Mindfulness Practices for Healing

Mindfulness is a practice rooted in the present moment. It invites you to observe your thoughts and feelings without judgment, creating a space where awareness and acceptance flourish. This approach can be transformative, particularly when healing from past traumas. Mindfulness encourages a break from the cycle of reliving past events or worrying about the future by focusing on the here and now. It offers a respite from the constant chatter of the mind, allowing you to experience life with clarity and calmness. Mindfulness also plays a role in stress reduction, helping to soothe the nervous system and foster a sense of peace. This practice isn't about changing your thoughts but your relationship with them, cultivating a state where you can navigate life's challenges with grace and resilience.

To incorporate mindfulness into your daily routine, consider starting with simple exercises that anchor you in the present. Deep breathing exercises are an excellent way to begin. Find a quiet space, sit comfortably, and take a slow, deep breath through your nose, allowing your abdomen to expand. Hold for a moment, then exhale slowly through your mouth. Repeat this cycle several times, focusing solely on the sensation of your breath. This practice calms the mind and regulates the body's stress response. Another effective technique is body scan meditation, where you systematically focus on each part of your body, observing any sensations or tension without trying to change them. This meditation can increase body awareness and release physical stress. Mindful walking, too, can be a moving meditation. As you walk, pay close attention to the rhythm of your footsteps, the feeling of the ground beneath you, and the surrounding sounds and smells. These exercises help ground you, offering a counterbalance to the emotional turbulence that often accompanies trauma.

The benefits of mindfulness extend beyond the momentary relief; they foster long-term emotional regulation and self-awareness. Practicing mindfulness teaches you to observe your emotions without being swept away. This detachment allows you to respond rather than react, enhancing your ability to handle stress and reducing the likelihood of emotional outbursts. Increased self-awareness emerges as you become more attuned to your thoughts and feelings, uncovering patterns and triggers that may have previously gone unnoticed. This awareness is empowering, providing insight into your behaviors and guiding you toward healthier responses. Over time, mindfulness strengthens your resilience, equipping you with the tools to navigate life's ups and downs with equanimity.

Let's consider Melissa, who struggled with anxiety following a traumatic event. She found solace in mindfulness practices, particularly deep breathing, which became her anchor during heightened stress. By focusing on her breath, Melissa could calm her racing thoughts and return to a balanced state. Her experience illustrates the power of mindfulness in managing anxiety and fostering emotional balance.

If you are interested in trying a guided body scan meditation, here is a simple script: Begin by lying comfortably. Close your eyes and take a few deep breaths. Inhale a deep breath in through your nose over 4 seconds, then release your breath over 8 seconds through your mouth. Start at the top of your head, noticing any sensations. Visualize relaxation with each part of your body and be aware as you gradually move your attention down to your neck, shoulders, arms, and so on until you reach your toes. As you scan, notice feelings, tension, or relaxation without judgment.

This practice helps cultivate a deeper connection with your body and promotes relaxation. Integrating these mindfulness techniques into your life opens the door to healing and growth, allowing emotional wounds to mend with compassion and awareness.

10.3 Creating a Safe Emotional Space

Imagine what it feels like to share your deepest fears and dreams without the dread of judgment or criticism. The essence of a safe emotional space is a haven in your relationship where vulnerability is met with understanding and support. In this setting, both partners feel safe expressing their feelings, knowing their emotions are understood with care instead of criticism. A safe emotional space allows you to be your true self, free from the fear of repercussions. It's the space to openly share your worries about a new job or lingering insecurities from past experiences without fearing being dismissed or ridiculed.

Empathy plays a pivotal role in establishing this sanctuary. It involves deeply understanding and validating each other's feelings, conveying that you genuinely care. When you actively listen to your partner, you do so without interrupting or jumping to conclusions. This practice fosters a sense of being honestly heard and understood. For instance, when your partner shares a tough day at work, responding with empathy—perhaps acknowledging their frustration and offering support—can significantly enhance emotional safety. Active listening is not just about hearing words; it's about understanding the emotions behind them. This attentive engagement makes your partner feel valued and respected, reinforcing the trust crucial for a healthy relationship.

To cultivate such an environment, you can start with some practical steps. Establishing ground rules for respectful communication is a good beginning. Agree on practices like not interrupting each other during conversations and taking turns to express your viewpoints. Patience and understanding during emotional exchanges help maintain composure, even when emotions run high. Consider agreeing to take breaks if discussions become too intense, allowing time for reflection and calm before continuing the conversation. These practices create a framework where emotional exchanges are constructive rather than destructive, reassuring both partners that their feelings are safe.

Consider the story of Maria and Diego, who often found themselves in heated arguments, leaving both feeling misunderstood. They decided to implement a rule: when one spoke, the other would listen without interruption, offering reflections only after the other had finished. Over time, this practice transformed their dynamic. Maria felt safe sharing her fears about their future, knowing Diego would respond with empathy rather than defensiveness. Diego, in turn, felt more connected and appreciated as they navigated their challenges together. Their increased emotional intimacy resulted from creating a safe space where both could express their true selves without fear of judgment.

Reflection Section: Cultivating Emotional Safety

Reflect on a recent conversation where you felt judged or misunderstood. Consider how a safe emotional space could have changed the interaction. Write down three ways you can create such a space in your relationship. These insights will guide you in fostering deeper emotional connections with your partner.

10.4 Trust-Building Activities

Imagine trust in a relationship as a garden. It requires regular care, attention, and nurturing to flourish. Trust-building activities are the tools that help tend to this garden, ensuring it grows strong and resilient. These activities enhance mutual trust and connection, encouraging teamwork and collaboration between partners. They provide opportunities to engage in joint projects or challenges, where you and your partner work together towards a common goal. This collaboration fosters a sense of unity and strengthens the emotional bond that underpins your relationship. Whether tackling a home improvement project, planning a weekend getaway, or simply trying a new hobby together, these activities build a foundation of trust that can withstand time.

There are countless activities that couples can engage in to build trust, such as collaborative problem-solving exercises and working together on a puzzle or escape room, which require communication and reliance on each other's strengths. Trust falls and physical support activities, like rock climbing or tandem biking, challenge you physically and emotionally, requiring you to lean on your partner and provide support. Cooking a complex meal together can be a fun and rewarding way to practice teamwork, planning, dividing tasks, and communicating effectively to achieve a delicious outcome. While varied, these activities share a common goal: to deepen your connection and reinforce the trust essential for a healthy relationship.

The benefits of regularly engaging in trust-building activities are manifold. They strengthen emotional bonds, creating a sense of closeness and security between partners. When you consistently engage in these activities, you build a reservoir of positive experiences and memories that reinforce your trust in each other. This increased sense of security and reliability translates into greater relationship satisfaction and a more resilient partnership. Consider setting aside time for a weekly trust-building activity night. This dedicated time allows you to focus on each other, away from the distractions of daily life. Whether you try a new activity or revisit an old favorite, the key is to be present and engaged with your partner, nurturing the trust that forms the foundation of your relationship.

Take, for example, the story of Mia and Leo. They found themselves drifting apart, overwhelmed by the demands of work and family. Determined to reconnect, they decided to try adventure sports together, starting with tandem kayaking. The experience required them to communicate and rely on each other's strengths, strengthening their bond and reigniting their connection. Over time, they incorporated other trust-building activities into their routine, such as attending dance classes and volunteering as a team. Through these shared experiences, they improved their relationship and discovered new facets of each other, deepening their understanding and appreciation. Mia reflects on their journey: "Taking time to engage in activities that require us to work together has transformed our relationship. We've learned to trust each other in ways we never thought possible, and our connection has never been stronger." This testament highlights the profound impact of regular trust-building exercises on relationship stability, creating a foundation of trust that endures.

10.5 Handling Jealousy and Insecurity

Jealousy and insecurity often walk hand in hand, casting long shadows over relationships. These feelings usually stem from past experiences and traumas that shape our emotional responses. Consider, for instance, the lingering effects of infidelity in a previous relationship. Such experiences can seed doubts, making it difficult to trust again fully. Fear of abandonment or betrayal can also take root, leading to constant vigilance. This fear is not unfounded; it's a protective mechanism developed over time. However, when unchecked, it can stifle the very connection it seeks to protect. It's crucial to understand these roots to address the feelings effectively.

Managing jealousy and insecurity requires deliberate action and understanding. One of the initial steps is to open lines of communication. Expressing fears openly with your partner can demystify them and reduce their power. This doesn't mean unloading all concerns at once but gradually sharing what weighs on your mind. Building self-confidence is equally important. When you cultivate a sense of self-worth, the insecurities lose their grip. Engaging in activities that reinforce your strengths can bolster this self-assurance. For example, a partner who feels insecure about their career might focus on professional development or hobbies that provide fulfillment. By nurturing your confidence, you build a foundation that supports a healthier relationship.

Supporting a partner grappling with jealousy or insecurity demands patience and empathy. Offering reassurance can be impactful. It is unnecessary to involve grand gestures but to be consistent and genuine where affirmations matter. Show understanding and validate their feelings without judgment. Avoid behaviors triggering their insecurities, such as secretive actions or dismissive comments. It's about creating an environment where they feel safe and valued. Consider the impact of consistent open communication. When a partner knows they can express their concerns without fear of ridicule, it fosters trust and understanding. Reassurance becomes a gentle reminder that they are loved and valued, cementing your bond.

Let's look at a couple who faced the specter of jealousy head-on. Sarah and James found themselves caught in frequent arguments fueled by Sarah's fear of infidelity. They decided to seek therapy, where they could explore these insecurities in a safe space. Through guided conversations, Sarah learned to articulate her fears without accusation, while James discovered ways to reassure her without feeling defensive. Over time, their relationship transformed. Sarah's testimonial reveals the shift: "We found a deeper connection by addressing our insecurities. Our communication improved, and I learned to trust James and myself." Their experience showcases the power of confronting insecurities and turning obstacles into stepping stones toward growth.

In summary, jealousy and insecurity are natural but can be navigated with understanding and effort. Recognizing one's roots, fostering open communication, building self-worth, and offering reassurance play pivotal roles. Addressing these feelings strengthens your relationship and paves the way for deeper connections and greater emotional intimacy. As we move forward, remember that handling jealousy and insecurity is not about eliminating them but managing them to enrich your relationship, setting the stage for continued growth and understanding in the chapters ahead.

Professional therapy can be transformative in healing past traumas. It helps individuals understand how trauma affects their relationships, manage intense emotions, rebuild trust, and improve communication and boundaries. Therapy also aids in reshaping self-worth, allowing individuals to feel deserving of positive connections, and equips them with resilience strategies for future relationship challenges.

Chapter 11

Enhancing Emotional Intelligence

Have you ever encountered a conversation where the other person's emotions ran deep, yet words seemed inadequate to capture the moment? You felt their joy, pain, or frustration as your own. This essence of Empathy is a cornerstone of emotional intelligence that transcends mere understanding. Empathy allows us to connect profoundly, creating bonds that foster mutual respect and trust. It's about feeling what is being. Empathy acts as a bridge in relationships, facilitating communication and fostering emotional intimacy. It's this capacity to step into another's shoes that enables us to build relationships that are not only resilient but deeply fulfilling.

Understanding and sharing the feelings of others is at the heart of Empathy. It's about more than just acknowledging someone's emotions; it's about truly feeling them. When your partner is navigating a tough time, Empathy allows you to provide support that feels genuine and meaningful. It's not about offering solutions or advice but about being present and validating their emotions. Empathy builds deeper emotional connections by showing others their feelings are seen and valued. This level of understanding is crucial for maintaining healthy relationships, as it creates an environment where both partners feel safe to express themselves without fear of judgment or dismissal.

Enhancing empathy skills is a journey that requires intentional practice and openness. One effective way to develop Empathy is through active listening exercises. These exercises focus entirely on the speaker, absorbing their words, tone, and body language. It means resisting the urge to interrupt or formulate a response while they are speaking. Instead, you aim to understand their perspective fully. Perspective-taking practices also play a significant role in developing Empathy. Empathy involves consciously considering how a situation might feel from another person's point of view. By putting yourself in your partner's shoes during conflicts, you see the issue through their eyes, fostering a deeper understanding and reducing defensiveness.

The benefits of empathy in relationships are profound. Increased emotional intimacy is one of the most significant outcomes. When partners feel understood and supported, they are likelier to open up and share their innermost thoughts and feelings. This openness strengthens the emotional bond and enhances trust. Empathy also leads to better conflict resolution. You can navigate conflicts constructively by approaching disagreements with an empathetic mindset. Instead of focusing on winning an argument, the goal becomes understanding each other's perspectives and finding a resolution that respects both parties' feelings. This change in strategy has the power to revolutionize how we handle conflicts, ultimately resulting in more harmonious and fulfilling relationships.

Consider the story of Rachel and Steve, a couple who struggled with communication in their relationship. They often found themselves in heated arguments, each unable to see the other's point of view. Recognizing the need for change, they decided to enhance their empathy skills. Rachel learned to tune into Steve's feelings more effectively through active listening exercises and perspective-taking practices. She discovered that his frustration often stemmed from feeling unheard.

Similarly, Steve realized that Rachel's concerns were valid and deserved acknowledgment. This newfound empathy allowed them to approach conflicts with compassion and understanding. Over time, their relationship transformed. They began to resolve disagreements more peacefully, leading to a stronger emotional connection and increased relationship satisfaction.

Testimonials from individuals who have successfully enhanced their empathy skills further illustrate its positive impact. One couple shared, "Empathy was the missing piece in our relationship. We've grown closer than ever by learning to listen and understand each other's emotions." Another individual recounted, "Practicing Empathy has changed how I interact with loved ones. It's improved my relationships and made me a better friend and partner." These stories highlight the transformative power of Empathy. When nurtured, it's a skill that can enrich your relationships and contribute to a more connected and harmonious life.

11.2 Emotional Regulation Techniques

Managing your emotions is like having a personal GPS for your feelings, guiding you through the complex terrain of relationships and daily interactions. Emotional regulation is the ability to manage and healthily respond to your emotions. It involves recognizing what you feel, understanding why, and choosing how to express those feelings constructively. Its significance lies in maintaining emotional balance and fostering healthy relationships. When you regulate your emotions effectively, you prevent emotional outbursts that can strain or damage your relationships. Picture an argument spiraling out of control—voices raised, words hurled like weapons. Now imagine breathing deeply, allowing your mind to clear and your heart rate to slow. This simple act can transform the conversation's trajectory, turning potential conflict into an opportunity for understanding.

There are several practical methods to help regulate your emotions effectively. Deep breathing exercises are a powerful tool. When you're in the midst of a heated discussion, taking slow, deliberate breaths can help calm your nervous system. This pause lets you approach the situation clearly, reducing the likelihood of saying something you regret. Cognitive reappraisal is another technique that involves reframing negative thoughts. For example, if your partner's criticism stings, view it as constructive feedback rather than a personal attack. This shift in perspective can change how you react, enabling you to respond with openness rather than defensiveness. Practicing these techniques helps build emotional resilience, equipping you to gracefully handle life's ups and downs.

The impact of emotional regulation on relationships is profound. Reducing the frequency and intensity of conflicts creates a more stable and harmonious environment. Emotional stability fosters trust and security, as partners know they can rely on each other to handle disagreements calmly. This stability also opens the door to deeper emotional connections, as both partners feel safe to express themselves without fear of explosive reactions. Imagine a relationship where conflicts are met with Empathy and understanding instead of anger and frustration. This environment encourages open dialogue and mutual respect, strengthening the bond between partners. When you regulate your emotions effectively, you improve your relationship dynamics and enhance your well-being.

Consider the story of Lisa, who struggled with managing her anger. Every disagreement with her spouse seemed to escalate into a full-blown argument. Realizing the toll it was taking on her marriage, Lisa decided to try mindfulness practices to help manage her emotions. She began with deep breathing exercises, practicing them daily to cultivate a sense of calm. Over time, she noticed a remarkable difference. During a tense conversation, she paused, took a few deep breaths, and responded thoughtfully rather than reactively. This shift in approach surprised her spouse, who responded with similar composure. Their conversations became more productive, and their connection became deeper. Lisa's case illustrates the impact of emotional regulation on conflict resolution and the general harmony within a relationship.

Testimonials from those who have embraced emotional regulation highlight its positive effects. One individual shared, "Learning to regulate my emotions has changed my life. My relationships are stronger, and I feel more in control." Another person noted, "Before, I felt like a passenger in my emotions. Now, I can steer them toward what benefits me and the people I care about." These stories underscore the power of emotional regulation to enhance relationship harmony. Taking control of your emotional responses creates a more peaceful and fulfilling life where relationships thrive, and personal growth flourishes.

11.3 Understanding Emotional Triggers

At some point, we've all experienced that sudden, overwhelming wave of emotion where a seemingly minor event stirs up intense feelings. These emotional triggers are specific events or situations that provoke strong emotional reactions. Understanding them is crucial for emotional management. Imagine a situation where you feel neglected by a loved one. This can trigger anger or hurt, especially if past experiences have left a mark. Recognizing these triggers is the first step toward managing them. It's about identifying what sets off these emotions and why they have such power over us. By understanding your triggers, you gain insight into your emotional responses, allowing you to react more thoughtfully rather than impulsively.

To identify your emotional triggers, start by keeping a trigger journal. Document situations that evoke strong emotions, noting the context and your reactions. This practice helps you see patterns and pinpoint specific triggers. Reflective exercises, such as meditation or quiet contemplation, can also be beneficial. Take time to consider recent events that have stirred your emotions. What was the common thread? Were there specific words or actions that heightened your response? By delving into these details, you gain clarity on what affects you most. For instance, you might realize that feeling unheard in conversations consistently leads to frustration. This awareness is a powerful tool, enabling you to predict and prepare for these situations in the future.

Managing emotional triggers means developing coping strategies that work for you effectively. One approach is to communicate your triggers to those close to you. Sharing your insights with your partner or friends can foster understanding and support. It allows them to be aware of your sensitivities and adjust their behavior accordingly. Additionally, grounding techniques can help you stay present during triggering events and focus on your breath, observe your surroundings, or engage your senses to anchor yourself in the moment. By practicing these techniques, you build resilience, reducing the impact of triggers on your emotional state. Imagine facing a situation that typically triggers anxiety. You remain calm and centered by employing grounding techniques, transforming your response from reactive to proactive.

Consider the story of James, who faced frequent conflicts in his relationship due to his strong emotional reactions. Through counseling, James began to recognize that his anger often stemmed from feeling undervalued at work. By identifying this trigger, he could communicate his needs more clearly to his partner. This understanding allowed him to approach conflicts with a calmer demeanor, reducing the frequency and intensity of their arguments. James's experience highlights the power of understanding and managing emotional triggers. It shows how self-awareness can transform personal well-being and relationship dynamics.

Testimonials from others who have mastered their emotional triggers offer further encouragement. One person shared, "Identifying my triggers was like finding a missing piece of the puzzle. I used to feel overwhelmed by my emotions, but now I have the tools to manage them." Another individual noted, "Discussing my triggers with my partner has changed everything. We communicate better, and my relationships are stronger because of it." These stories underscore the benefits of addressing emotional triggers head-on. By embracing this self-awareness, you pave the way for healthier interactions and deeper connections.

As you continue exploring the complexities of your emotional landscape, remember that this journey is personal. Emotional triggers are deeply rooted in our experiences and perceptions. They offer valuable insights into our emotional makeup, guiding us toward greater self-understanding and emotional intelligence. By identifying and managing these triggers, you enhance your ability to navigate life's challenges with grace and resilience. This chapter has provided tools to help you achieve this, inviting you to explore your emotions with curiosity and compassion.

In closing, understanding, and learning to manage emotional triggers is vital to emotional intelligence. It empowers you to control your emotional responses, leading to more harmonious relationships and personal growth. Integrating these practices into your life will make you better equipped to handle whatever challenges come your way, paving the path for continued emotional development.

Chapter 12

Practical Applications and Exercises

Remember the last time you tried to solve a puzzle? You spread all the pieces across the table, unsure where to start but confident that with patience, each piece would eventually find its place. Relationships often resemble intricate puzzles, where each moment and interaction is a piece that contributes to a larger picture. This chapter invites you to explore common relationship scenarios like puzzles waiting to be solved. By examining these scenarios closely, you can learn to identify the root causes of issues, communicate effectively to resolve misunderstandings and embrace flexibility for a harmonious relationship.

12.2 Real-Life Scenarios and Solutions

It's common to find yourself in a heated discussion about finances, where stress and emotions run high. Here is an example of a couple, Alex and Jamie, who repeatedly clash over their spending habits. Alex prefers saving for the future, while Jamie enjoys the spontaneity of splurging on experiences. These opposing views can quickly escalate into conflict if not managed thoughtfully. The key lies in identifying the root cause of the issue. For Alex and Jamie, the underlying problem isn't just about money—it's about security versus adventure. Understanding this allows them to address the core of the conflict rather than just the surface disagreement.

Communication plays a pivotal role in resolving these financial misunderstandings. By calmly setting aside time to discuss their financial goals and priorities, Alex and Jamie can align their expectations. They might create a joint budget with room for savings and discretionary spending. This compromise acknowledges both of their needs, fostering a sense of teamwork rather than competition. It's crucial to approach such discussions with an open mind, ready to listen and adapt. Realizing that flexibility can transform disagreements into opportunities for growth is essential for long-term success.

Misunderstandings in communication are another common scenario that can strain relationships. Consider Emma and James, who often misinterpret each other's intentions. Sarah feels distant when James seems distracted, while James misreads Emma's silence as disinterest. This miscommunication creates a cycle of confusion and frustration. They must identify the root cause to break this cycle: differing communication styles. Emma thrives on verbal affirmations, while James expresses himself through actions. Recognizing these differences allows them to communicate more effectively.

A step-by-step approach can help resolve such misunderstandings. Emma and James might dedicate time each week to discussing their feelings openly, using "I" statements to express their needs without assigning blame. This practice encourages vulnerability and fosters understanding. Acknowledging their unique communication styles, they can adjust their interactions to meet each other's needs better. Flexibility is critical, as it allows them to adapt their approach based on feedback and outcomes, ensuring that their relationship continues to evolve positively.

Navigating different social needs is another puzzle many couples face. Picture Emma and Leo, who have contrasting social preferences. Emma enjoys lively gatherings, while Leo finds solace in quieter settings. This difference can lead to tension if not addressed with Empathy and understanding. By identifying the root cause—Emma's need for social stimulation versus Leo's need for quiet reflection—they can find a balance that respects their needs.

Emma and Leo can explore step-by-step solutions that cater to their social preferences to achieve this balance. They might agree to alternate between attending social events and spending quiet evenings at home. This compromise ensures that both partners feel valued and respected. Open communication about their needs and feelings allows them to adapt their plans based on feedback, fostering a sense of partnership. Flexibility is essential, enabling them to embrace different approaches and find creative solutions that strengthen their bond.

Case Study: A Major Misunderstanding Resolved

Consider the story of Cindy and Rob, whose relationship was on the brink due to a significant misunderstanding. Rob assumed Cindy's silence during stressful times meant she was upset with him, while Cindy believed Rob's need for space signaled withdrawal. This misinterpretation led to a growing emotional chasm. By identifying the root cause of their misunderstanding—differing expressions of stress—they were able to address the issue directly. Through open dialogue and vulnerability, they learned to communicate their needs and intentions more clearly. This case study is a powerful reminder that effective communication and flexibility can bridge gaps, transforming misunderstandings into opportunities for deeper connection.

Testimonials from couples who have successfully applied structured solutions highlight the transformative power of these approaches. For instance, Emma and James share how their relationship improved once they learned to communicate openly and adapt their interactions. They emphasize the importance of patience and understanding, noting that their bond grew stronger as they embraced flexibility and addressed misunderstandings with Empathy. These testimonials underscore the value of practical solutions and their positive impact on relationships.

12.3 Interactive Exercises for Couples

Engaging in interactive exercises with your partner is like giving your relationship a tune-up. These activities are fun and profoundly enriching, promoting teamwork and cooperation. Imagine the bond you can strengthen when you work together towards a common goal. When you engage in these exercises, you create a space where open communication and connection can flourish. Picture an exercise where you practice active listening. You and your partner share thoughts while the other listens without interrupting. It's a simple yet profound way to ensure that both of you feel heard and valued, laying a foundation for deeper understanding and Empathy.

There's a variety of exercises you can try, each targeting different aspects of your relationship. Trust-building games are a fantastic start. Consider an exercise where you and your partner guide each other blindfolded through a simple obstacle course, relying solely on verbal instructions. This activity requires trust and communication, reinforcing your ability to rely on one another. Communication role-plays can also be enlightening. In a controlled setting, you can practice resolving conflicts by acting out scenarios and experimenting with different approaches to see what works best. Then, there are emotional intimacy exercises, like expressing and receiving appreciation. Imagine sitting across from your partner, sharing what you admire about them, and receiving their words with gratitude. This exercise can foster a sense of warmth and closeness, reminding you of the qualities that drew you together.

Remember, conducting these exercises effectively and setting the stage is essential. Start by creating a comfortable and distraction-free environment. Turn off your phones, dim the lights if it helps, and ensure you're both willing participants. It's essential to approach these activities with an open mind and a shared commitment to growth. For a trust-building game, start by explaining the rules clearly. If you're trying the obstacle course, ensure that the path is safe and free of hazards. Blindfolding, while the other provides guidance, then switches roles to experience both perspectives. The key is to listen carefully, communicate clearly, and support each other throughout the process.

Real-life examples highlight the transformative potential of these exercises. Take the story of David and Laura, who felt their relationship had hit a plateau. They decided to try a series of trust-building games, including the blindfolded obstacle course. Through laughter and occasional missteps, they discovered an increased sense of trust and reliance on each other. David reflected, "It was incredible to realize how much I had to trust Laura's voice. It reminded me of the importance of clear communication." Their experience is a testament to how such exercises reignite trust and excitement in a relationship.

Another couple, Sam and Emily, found communication role-plays particularly beneficial. They often clashed over minor misunderstandings, leading to unnecessary tension. By acting out potential conflicts in a structured environment, they could experiment with different ways of expressing themselves. Emily shared, "Role-playing allowed us to see how our words and actions affected each other. It was eye-opening and helped us approach real-life disagreements more constructively." Their testimony illustrates how these exercises enhance connection and understanding, transforming how partners relate.

Engaging in interactive exercises strengthens your relationship and provides valuable insights into each other's perspectives. Participating actively and sharing these moments creates a reservoir of positive experiences to draw upon during challenging times. These exercises are more than just activities; they are opportunities to deepen your connection, build trust, and cultivate a more harmonious partnership.

12.4 Continuous Improvement and Learning

In relationships, just like in any other significant aspect of life, there are always alternatives to remaining stagnant if growth is the goal. Relationships thrive on the continuous effort to adapt, learn, and evolve. It's not just about maintaining the status quo; it's about fostering an environment where both partners feel encouraged to grow individually and together. Think of it as a shared commitment to personal and mutual development. By continuously updating relationship goals, you create a dynamic where the relationship is alive and thriving rather than just existing. This proactive approach prevents the relationship from becoming monotonous, injecting vitality and excitement into your shared life. For instance, set a goal to explore new hobbies together or to improve communication skills. These goals keep the relationship fresh and focused, providing a shared sense of purpose. Laughter is also vital for couples to consider because it strengthens emotional bonds and helps create a positive, joyful atmosphere in the relationship. Sharing moments of humor can relieve tension during stressful times, fostering a sense of closeness and understanding. Additionally, laughter encourages open communication and mutual appreciation, helping couples navigate challenges with a lighter, more connected mindset.

Continuous learning is the backbone of this growth. Regular self-reflection allows you to critically assess your role in the relationship, identifying areas where you excel and others where improvement is needed. This self-awareness is crucial, as it forms the foundation for meaningful change. Seeking new resources and learning opportunities can also be transformative. Attending relationship workshops or seminars provides new perspectives and introduces you to techniques and insights you might have yet to consider. These experiences can be eye-opening, offering practical tools to enhance your relationship. Imagine attending a workshop focusing on emotional intelligence, where you learn how to understand and manage your emotions better. This newfound knowledge could drastically improve your interactions with your partner, leading to deeper emotional connections.

Feedback is an invaluable tool in this process of continuous improvement. Actively seeking your partner's input on relationship dynamics encourages an open dialogue that can uncover hidden concerns or unmet needs. It's about creating a safe space for honest communication where both partners feel comfortable sharing their thoughts and feelings. Being open to feedback means making changes based on what you learn.

This adaptability is a sign of strength, not weakness, and it shows a commitment to the relationship's health.

An example of this could be implementing a monthly review of your relationship's progress. During these reviews, you can discuss what's working well and what areas need attention. This practice keeps the relationship on track and reinforces your commitment to each other's happiness and growth.

Real-life examples abound of couples who have embraced continuous improvement to significant effect. Consider the story of Mark and Lisa, who regularly attended relationship workshops to enhance their connection. Through these workshops, they discovered new ways to communicate and resolve conflicts, significantly improving their relationship satisfaction. They found that the skills they learned applied to their romantic relationship and enriched other areas of their lives. Lisa mentioned how these workshops helped her communicate better with her colleagues, while Mark noted an improvement in his ability to handle stress. Their story is a testament to the positive impact that continuous learning can have on relationship dynamics.

Testimonials from other couples further illustrate the benefits of this approach. Sarah and Tom, for instance, shared how their relationship blossomed once they committed to ongoing learning. They participated in seminars and read books on relationship psychology, which gave them a deeper understanding of each other's needs and desires. This commitment to learning helped them navigate challenges with greater ease and Empathy. They emphasized how these experiences brought them closer, as they felt more connected and attuned to each other's emotional landscapes. Their journey highlights the transformative power of continuous improvement, strengthening the relationship and fostering a more profound sense of fulfillment and joy.

Embracing continuous improvement and learning enhances your relationship and enriches your personal growth. This chapter has explored the importance of ongoing effort and adaptability, offering actionable strategies and real-life examples to inspire your journey. As you integrate these practices into your relationship, you'll find that the rewards extend far beyond the immediate benefits, leading to a more vibrant, resilient, and fulfilling partnership. With this foundation, you are well-prepared to explore the next chapter, which delves into sustaining relationship health over time.

Chapter 13

Sustaining Relationship Health Over Time

Imagine the rhythm of a favorite song playing softly in the background of your life. Much like music, relationships require harmony and balance to thrive. Regular relationship check-ins can be the drumbeat that maintains this harmony, ensuring both partners move in sync. These check-ins are more than just a scheduled conversation; they are an opportunity to pause, reflect, and reconnect. By dedicating time to discuss the state of your relationship, you open the door to addressing issues before they snowball into larger conflicts. This practice ensures that both partners feel heard and valued, reinforcing the foundation of trust and understanding.

To make the most of these check-ins, it helps to follow a structured approach. Start by setting a regular time that suits you both—perhaps weekly or bi-weekly, depending on your needs. Treat this time as sacred, free from distractions like phones or television. Begin each session with positive reflections, acknowledging what went well in the relationship. This sets a constructive tone and reinforces positive behaviors. Next, discuss any concerns or issues that may have arisen. Approach these conversations with Empathy and a willingness to listen, aiming to understand your partner's perspective. Finally, set goals for improvement, identifying actionable steps to enhance your relationship. You both leave the conversation feeling empowered and aligned by concluding with a shared vision for the future.

To guide these check-ins, consider using specific questions that encourage open dialogue. Questions like "What went well in our relationship this week?" allow you to celebrate successes and express gratitude. Asking, "Is there anything that has been bothering you?" provides a safe space for voicing concerns, preventing resentment from building up. "How can we support each other better?" fosters collaboration and mutual support, strengthening your partnership. These questions facilitate meaningful conversations and deepen your connection, reminding you both of the love and commitment you share.

Real-life examples highlight the transformative power of regular check-ins. Take Sarah and Mike, who were drifting apart amidst their busy schedules. By committing to weekly check-ins, they discovered minor issues before they escalated, such as misunderstandings over household responsibilities. These sessions became a cornerstone of their relationship, enhancing their communication and Empathy. Sarah said, "I feel more connected and understood than ever." Their experience underscores the profound impact of regular check-ins, fostering a sense of unity and shared purpose.

Interactive Element: Reflection Exercise

Think about your current communication habits. Reflect on how often you and your partner engage in meaningful conversations about your relationship. Consider writing down three questions you'd like to ask during your next check-in. This exercise will help you approach the discussion with intention, ensuring you both feel heard and respected. As you engage in this practice, remember that the goal is to address challenges and celebrate your successes, nurturing a relationship that continues to grow and flourish.

13.2 Continued Personal Growth

Think of personal growth as a river flowing through your relationship's landscape, nourishing the soil and allowing both partners to flourish. Continual personal development is crucial for preventing stagnation. It keeps life vibrant and ensures that each person in the relationship feels fulfilled. When you pursue growth, you avoid the weariness of routine and predictability. This evolution fosters mutual respect. As you develop new skills or perspectives, your partner witnesses your transformation, deepening their admiration for you. This admiration reinforces the foundation of your relationship, keeping it strong and resilient.

To embrace personal growth, consider pursuing new hobbies or interests. This could be anything from taking up painting to learning a new language. Such activities enrich your life and provide fresh experiences to share with your partner. Engaging in lifelong learning can also be transformative. Courses and workshops offer a structured way to gain new knowledge and skills, keeping your mind active and engaged. Setting personal goals and milestones gives you something to strive for, creating a sense of purpose and achievement. Imagine enrolling in a new professional course that challenges and expands your horizons. This endeavor boosts your confidence and brings new energy into your relationship as you share your progress and insights with your partner.

Support from your partner plays a vital role in personal growth. Encouragement can be as simple as a kind word or as significant as helping you carve out time for your pursuits and celebrating achievements together, whether a promotion at work or mastering a new skill, creates shared joy and strengthens your bond. Providing emotional and practical support when needed, like offering to handle chores so your partner can study, reinforces the sense of teamwork and partnership. This mutual support ensures that both partners feel valued and understood, laying the groundwork for continued growth and connection.

Consider the story of Jack and Emily. When Jack decided to change careers, Emily stood by him, offering unwavering support. She celebrated each milestone with him, from completing courses to securing his first job in the new field. This journey brought them closer and ignited a new level of respect and admiration for one another. Emily's testimonial speaks volumes: "Supporting Jack through his career change strengthened our relationship in ways I never imagined. His growth inspired me to pursue my own goals." Their story highlights the profound impact of mutual encouragement and growth, illustrating how personal development can enhance relationship dynamics.

Reflection Section

Reflect on your personal growth journey. Consider what new skills or interests you'd like to explore. Write down three goals you want to achieve in the next year. Think about how you and your partner can support each other in these pursuits. This reflection will help you identify areas for growth and create a plan to pursue them, fostering a relationship that thrives on mutual support and admiration. As you share these insights with your partner, you engage in a dynamic process that enriches your individual lives and deepens your connection.

13.3 Mutual Appreciation Practices

In the framework of relationships, mutual appreciation is the vibrant thread that holds everything together. It's a gentle reminder that your efforts are valued, reinforcing positive behaviors and strengthening emotional bonds. When you express appreciation, you create an environment where love and support flourish. It is not about grand gestures but the everyday acknowledgments that weave a supportive atmosphere. Your relationship becomes a sanctuary where both partners feel cherished, fostering a positive environment that nurtures growth and connection. Regularly expressing appreciation lays the groundwork for a relationship that thrives on understanding and Empathy.

Practical ways to show appreciation can transform the mundane into moments of connection. Verbal affirmations are a powerful tool—simple yet profound. Telling your partner what you appreciate about them reinforces their strengths and builds their confidence. Compliments are not just about appearances; they can acknowledge efforts and small victories. Small acts of kindness also speak volumes. Preparing a favorite meal or taking over a chore shows you care about their comfort and happiness. Writing appreciation notes or letters offers a tangible reminder of your affection, allowing your partner to revisit your words whenever they need reassurance. Consider adopting a daily habit of expressing one thing you appreciate about your partner. It could be as simple as acknowledging their patience or praising their creativity. These actions, however small, accumulate to create a reservoir of goodwill and affection that sustains your relationship through challenges.

Cultivating a habit of appreciation requires intention and mindfulness. Start by setting reminders to express gratitude. You might place a sticky note on your mirror or set an alarm on your phone. These prompts ensure that appreciation becomes a regular practice rather than an occasional effort. Keeping a gratitude journal can also help you focus on the positive aspects of your relationship. Write down three things you appreciate about your partner each day. This practice reinforces your feelings and shifts your perspective to notice and celebrate the good in your partner. Practicing appreciation rituals, such as a weekly gratitude-sharing session, can deepen your connection. During these moments, take turns expressing what you appreciate about each other, creating a cycle of positivity and affirmation. These rituals remind you both of the love and support you share, reinforcing your bond and commitment.

Consider the story of Lucy and Dave, a couple who adopted daily affirmations to maintain positivity. Each morning, they shared one thing they appreciated about each other, setting a positive tone for the day. This practice became a cherished ritual, enhancing their communication and emotional connection. Lucy shared, "Knowing that Dave appreciates even the little things I do makes me feel valued and loved." Their experience highlights how consistent appreciation can transform a relationship, fostering a sense of security and satisfaction. Another couple, Jack and Maria, found that writing weekly appreciation letters strengthened their relationship. Maria noted, "Reading Jack's words reminds me of why we fell in love in the first place." These testimonials underscore the profound impact of consistent appreciation, illustrating its role in nurturing a healthy, happy relationship.

13.4 Keeping the Romance Alive

Keeping the romance alive in a relationship is like tending to a garden. It requires regular care and attention to ensure it doesn't wither. Romance prevents the creeping in of complacency. It keeps the emotional and physical connections strong, ensuring the spark doesn't fade. Romance is not just about grand gestures; it's about the little things that add excitement and novelty to your everyday lives. Whether it's a spontaneous hug or a thoughtful note left on the kitchen counter, these small acts remind your partner that they are cherished. By keeping romance at the forefront, you breathe life into your relationship, making it vibrant and fulfilling.

Consider planning surprise dates as a way to reignite the spark. These dates don't have to be extravagant. A simple picnic under the stars or a walk in the park can be just as special. Writing love letters or notes can also be incredibly romantic. In today's digital age, a handwritten note carries a unique charm. It shows thoughtfulness and effort, making your partner feel treasured. Creating special traditions, such as anniversary rituals, can also add a layer of sentimentality. You could revisit where you first met or cook a special meal together. These traditions become the glue that binds you, providing continuity and a shared history. Imagine surprising your partner with a weekend getaway. The anticipation and excitement of exploring a new place together can work wonders for your connection.

Integrating romance into daily life might seem challenging, but it's possible with some creativity. Start with your morning and evening routines. A gentle kiss or a warm embrace can set a positive tone for the day or night. Regularly scheduled date nights can also keep the romance alive.

These dates don't have to be elaborate; the key is consistency. Make it a point to set aside time for the two of you, free from distractions. Leaving their favorite treat in the fridge or sending an unexpected text and other small surprises can keep things exciting. Thoughtful acts show your partner that you're thinking of them, even amidst the busyness of life.

Real-life stories often best illustrate the impact of these romantic gestures. Take, for instance, a couple who revitalized their relationship through regular date nights. Initially, they struggled to find time for each other, but they rediscovered their connection by committing to a weekly date. It became a cherished ritual that strengthened their bond. Another couple found that spontaneous romantic gestures, like surprise flowers or a homemade dinner, brought them closer together. One partner shared, "These small surprises remind me that I'm loved and appreciated." Their experiences highlight how romance doesn't have to be grand to be meaningful. It's the consistent effort and thoughtfulness that indeed count.

Romance plays an indispensable role in sustaining relationship health over time. It wards off routine's dullness, enriching both emotional and physical connections. With romantic gestures, you nurture not just passion but also deeper bonds. As we conclude this chapter, remember that romance requires ongoing effort, but its rewards are profound. Next, we'll explore how to navigate life's transitions together, ensuring your relationship remains resilient and adaptable through all life's changes.

Conclusion

Key Takeaways

As you embark on this path to building and maintaining healthy relationships, I encourage you to embrace each step with an open heart and mind. Relationships are a continuous journey of growth, understanding, and love. They require patience, compassion, and a willingness to adapt. Celebrate your progress and be kind to yourself and your partner. No matter how small, every effort you make contributes to a stronger, more resilient relationship.

As you implement these insights, remember several key takeaways.

Key Takeaways:

- The Foundation of Healthy Relationships explained

- Relationships thrive on **mutual respect, trust, and communi-**

cation, which are the building blocks of long-lasting and meaningful connections.

- **Self-awareness and Emotional Intelligence**

- Cultivating **self-awareness** enhances empathy and emotional intelligence, allowing you to navigate complex situations with clarity and understanding.

- **Effective Communication**

- Learning to express your needs using "I" statements and practicing active listening transforms conflicts into opportunities for growth.

- **Attachment Styles and Personality Dynamics**

- Recognizing how **attachment styles** and **introvert-extrovert dynamics** influence interactions enables you to appreciate and manage different relationship dynamics.

- **Setting and Maintaining Boundaries**

- **Boundaries** are essential to preserving balance and respect. Understanding and communicating them clearly protects your well-being and ensures mutual respect in your relationships.

- **Emotional Intimacy**

- **Daily check-ins** and shared activities help to nurture emotional closeness, serving as anchors to keep you connected during life's challenges.

- **Balancing Independence and Togetherness**

- Supporting each other's interests while cherishing shared moments creates a healthy dynamic where independence and unity coexist harmoniously.

- **Breaking Toxic Patterns**

- Identifying and overcoming toxic behaviors empowers you to break free from harmful cycles and shape healthier relationship dynamics.

Next Steps: Now, it's time for Action!

Take Action

- Apply these principles to your relationships, starting with small, manageable steps. Reflect on areas where change is needed, and work on active listening, expressing your needs, and honoring boundaries.

- **Consistent Effort**

- Build emotional reconnection through regular check-ins, shared activities, and support for each other's growth. Relationships require **ongoing effort**—progress may be gradual, but every step counts.

- **Embrace the Journey** Relationships are a continuous journey of growth, patience, and love. Celebrate your progress, be kind to yourself, and enjoy the process of building stronger, more resilient connections.

As a coach and life enthusiast, I have witnessed the transformative power of dedication and perseverance. As a rider and horse, you can cultivate trust and understanding in your relationships by building trust through consistent effort. May this book serve as a guide and inspiration. Let it remind you that the path to healthy relationships is not solitary but shared, celebrated, and cherished with those you love. Embrace the path ahead with courage, dedication, optimism, and perseverance. Your desired relationships are well within reach, knowing that every step brings you closer to the fulfilling connections you seek.

Resources

1 2 Elements of Healthy Relationships. Johns Hopkins University Well-being

The Importance of Emotional Intimacy in Your Relationship. Anxiety and Stress Center

10 Ways to Practice Self-Awareness in Relationships. Marriage.com

The Power of Emotional Intelligence in Relationships. CARE Clinics

The Enneagram Types in Relationship. Dr. David Daniels

The Challenges of the Introvert-Extrovert Relationship. Introvert Dear

Attachment Theory: Bowlby and Ainsworth's. Verywell Mind

Why Anxious and Avoidant Attachment Attract Each Other. Psychology Today

The Importance of Emotional Intelligence(Incl. Quotes). Positive Psychology

What Self-Awareness Really Is (and How to Cultivate It). Harvard Business Review

Mindfulness and Emotion Regulation: Insights from Research. NCBI

The Importance of Empathy in Relationships. Array Behavioral Care

7 Active Listening Techniques For Better Communication. Verywell Mind

How to Use "I" Statements: A Clear Guide. First Session

Body Language and Nonverbal Communication. HelpGuide

The Art of a Heartfelt Apology. Harvard Health

The 10 Most Common Sources of Conflict in Relationships. Psychology Today

Manage Conflict: Repair and De-Escalate. Gottman Institute

6 Steps to Creating a Win-Win Solution. CMOE

How Couples Can Rebuild Trust in a Relationship. Verywell Mind

The Importance of Personal Boundaries. Psych Central

How to Be Assertive and Set Healthy Boundaries. Welldoing

How to Respect Other People's Boundaries. Verywell Mind

How to Deal with People Who Violate Boundaries. Counseling Recovery

The Importance of a Weekly Check-in for Couples. The Heart of the Matter Counseling

7 Simple Exercises To Strengthen Your Relationship. New York Times

85 Deep Conversation Starters for Couples. Brides

Improve Your Relationship by Paying Attention to "Bids". Gottman Institute

10 Techniques for Couples to Align Relationships and Time. Marriage.com

The Importance of Personal Space in Relationships. Grace Therapy Austin

Supporting Your Spouse's Interests (Even the Ones that Bug You). Engaged Marriage

Toxic Relationships: Signs and How to Heal. Women's Health

Effects of Emotional Abuse on Your Brain, Relationships. Psych Central

6 Tips for Ending a Cycle of Unhealthy Relationships. Psychology Today

17 Self-Awareness Activities and Exercises (+Test). Positive Psychology

Emotional Baggage: Symptoms, Causes, & How to Cope. Choosing Therapy

Trauma-Informed Mindfulness: A Guide. Psych Central

15 Journal Prompts for Inner Healing. Robyn Liechti

28 Best Trauma Therapy Activities to Help You Heal. NYC Therapeutic Wellness

The Importance of Transparency in a Relationship. Paired

7 Ways to Create Emotional Safety in Your Relationship. Psych Central

12 Proven Trust-Building Exercises to Repair Relationships. River Oaks Psychology

How to Deal With Jealousy and Insecurity in a Relationship. Verywell Mind

How to Develop Empathy in Relationships. Verywell Mind

Effect of Emotion Regulation on Mental Health of Couples. Wiley Online Library

How to Identify and Manage Your Emotional Triggers. Healthline

Empathy in Relationships Is the Key to Connection. Abby Medcalf

What Is Relationship Conflict? Definition, Examples. Pollack Peacebuilding

7 Relationship Problems and How to Solve Them. WebMD

17 Communication Exercises for Couples Therapy. Talkspace

How to Apply Continuous Improvement to Build Relationships at Work. [Training Magazine](https://trainingmag.com/how-to-apply-continuous-improvement-to

About the Author

Laurie Grist is a best-selling author and licensed equestrian coach with over three decades of experience. As an accomplished athlete, she finds joy in inspiring others to reach for their dreams and goals. Having a strong background in sales, life coaching, and women's leadership skills, Laurie's journey embodies a commitment to drive and empower individuals on their paths to success, both personally and professionally, through her writing. Her legacy offers an enduring invitation to readers to pursue their aspirations with determination and embrace the transformative power of self-discovery.

Laurie Grist's multifaceted life includes her professional endeavors and her passion for adventure and family. As a competitive ATV racer, Laurie has tasted victory on the track, clinching the prestigious title of Ontario Ladies Champion #CMRCATV. Her love for adrenaline-fueled sports isn't just a solo pursuit; it's a family affair. Alongside her children,

Laurie had formed a formidable racing team, dominating the ATV racing scene and collecting numerous awards. This shared passion for adventure and competition served as a source of inspiration and motivation for her kids, along with many other sports they were active in such as hockey and equestrian sports.

Laurie treasures the moments spent with family, horses and her many pets. Laurie is grateful for her supportive family, the love of her life, and her amazing friends who have inspired her along the way.

Connect with Laurie

LinkedIn:

LINKEDIN

Instagram:

INSTA-
GRAM